Thomas and the Lantern

Written by: Kevin H. Grenier

Illustrated by: Terry Herb

Perieco Publishing

© Copyright 2010 – Perieco Publishing

All rights reserved. This book is protected by the copyright laws of the United States of America. This book may not be copied or reprinted for commercial gain or profit. The use of short quotations or occasional page copying for personal use is permitted and encouraged.

Paperback Edition
ISBN 10: 0-9822159-9-1
ISBN 13: 978-0-9822159-9-9

Hardcover Edition
ISBN 10: 0-9822159-7-5
ISBN 13: 978-0-9822159-7-5

Library of Congress Control Number: 2009913578

Perieco Publishing
www.periecopublishing.com

This book is dedicated to our children

Taylor, who is a loyal, compassionate friend and an honest worker. You have a heart of gold and we are proud of the man you've become!

Emily, our voracious reader, who writes fantastic stories and songs, and dances beautifully. You bring us great delight!

Levi, who can run fast, fix anything and is always eager and ready to join me for an adventure. You are a true carrier of joy!

Daniel, who is a lover of justice, jumps like a flea and can do math in his head faster than a calculator. You are adorable!

Samuel, a fun-loving little boy who is always climbing something and has the best laugh in the world. You are a treasure!

Anna, our last bundle of joy, with a smile that won't quit, an eagerness to help and a ready supply of 'great ideas.' You are wonderful!

You are each a blessing and a joy!

In memory of Herman Holmes

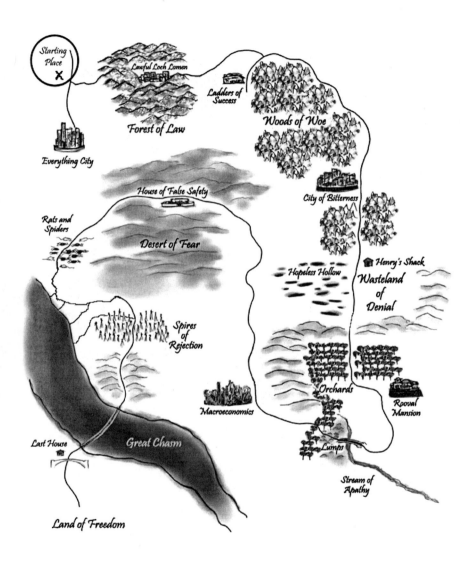

The Land of Bondage

Table of Contents

Preface 1
The Mysterious Visitor 3
Everything City 9
Shoveling Coal 15
The Forest of Law 21
Lawful Loch Lomen 27
Jimmy in Jail 33
The Supreme Court 39
The Ladder of Success 47
Climbing the Ladder 53
Helmud and the Woods of Woe 61
Ball & Chain 67
Queen Juliana 75
Escape from the City of Bitterness 81
The Wasteland of Denial 87
Muddling Through 95
In the Pits 101
The Maze of Approval 107
Iced Tea 113
Wonderful Rest 119
Escape 125
A Busy Place 129
Break Time! 135
The City Falls Apart 141
Desert of Fear 145
House of False Safety 151
Museum of Fear 157
The Journey Continues 163
Spires of Rejection 169
The Great Chasm 177
The Crossing 183
The Last House 189
A Final Bid for Freedom 195
Going Home 201

Tablets of Elsdat

Preface

Long forgotten, the stone Tablets of Elsdat lay buried in a forest in the Land of Bondage. As the seasons passed, the tablets had been covered by dirt, tree roots and grass, obscuring their writings. Those who took the time, however, could still uncover the legends engraved on each tablet. The writings spoke of future times and past events, triumphs and disasters, victories and defeats.

Most important of all, there were the stories about the lantern-bearer, the one who would carry the Lantern of Elsdat from the Land of Bondage to the Land of Freedom. It was written that the lantern-bearer would one day bring freedom to the Land of Bondage.

For centuries, the Lantern of Elsdat had been kept in the castle of the Wizard of Freedom. It was his task to protect the lantern until the day that the lantern-bearer would begin his journey.

In the meantime, though, Thomas had to get up for school in three hours.

"You have been chosen."

I

The Mysterious Visitor

"Thomas!"

"Thomas!" the deep, rumbling voice repeated.

Nine-year-old Thomas rubbed his eyes and blinked. It was still night, yet a brilliant light streamed toward him from the foot of his bed. Squinting, the boy could just barely make out the figure of an old wizard.

Thomas knew he was a wizard because of his white beard and flowing robes. The boy shaded his eyes to get a better look. The wizard looked strong and his beard did little to hide his stern face.

"Thomas," the wizard repeated a third time. His face was now even more serious than at first.

"Y-y-yes," the boy answered. Thomas was beginning to wake up, although he wasn't so sure that he really was awake, there being a wizard at his bedside after all.

"You have been chosen," the wizard announced.

"Chosen? For what?"

"You have been chosen to be the lantern-bearer. You are to carry the Lantern of Elsdat from the Land of Bondage to the Land of Freedom."

None of that made any sense to Thomas. He didn't know what a Lantern of Elsdat was. He didn't know where the Land of Freedom was. In fact, he didn't even know what to make of this wizard. Perhaps, thought Thomas, I'm only dreaming.

"This is only a silly dream," he replied to the wizard. "Besides, I have to go to school in the morning. I don't have time for any Lantern of Eldisimor or whatever."

The wizard frowned at Thomas. "Be that as it may," he declared. Then he raised his wooden staff and waved it over Thomas' bed.

In an instant, Thomas found himself standing on a road that ran right by a forest. He was wearing his school clothes instead of pajamas, but that was the only thing that looked or felt familiar. The weather was warm and not at all like the blustery autumn days at home. Before him, the single lane road led out across a broad plain. Some distance ahead there was a city, but it didn't look like his hometown.

Thomas noticed a small backpack sitting beside him on the ground. When he peeked inside, he found a jacket and a lantern. As Thomas gazed at its brightly shining light, he was startled by the wizard as he spoke to Thomas once again.

"You must carry the Lantern of Elsdat into the Land of Freedom," the wizard commanded. "Guard it closely."

"Where did you come from?" Thomas demanded.

The wizard looked at Thomas very seriously.

"The legends foretell that you must make this journey," he replied solemnly. "It is a great distance to the Land of Freedom and you will face many dangers. So beware."

"Some places will claim to have freedom, but they will only lead to bondage," he continued. "There will also be those who will try to distract you from your quest. Don't be fooled. Keep going to the Land of Freedom."

"I don't want to go to the Land of Freedom," Thomas argued. "I want to go home."

The wizard gave Thomas a sobering look. "You must carry this lantern to the Land of Freedom. If you don't make it there, you will never be able to go home."

"But . . . ," Thomas objected.

It was too late. The wizard had already disappeared in a flash of light. The boy was left standing alone with no idea what to do next.

Almost immediately, Thomas saw a sign along the road just up ahead. Walking closer, he discovered that there were actually two small signs on a single pole. One sign pointed to the left and read:

Land of Freedom

Thomas' eyes followed the arrow. It directed him to take a narrow path down a slight hill and into a dark forest. It looked scary. Glancing back at the other sign, Thomas breathed a sigh of relief. It read:

Shortcut

"*Anything would be better than that forest,*" he thought to himself.

The shortcut sign pointed down the smooth, paved road that led to the city. Even from so far away, Thomas was able to make out its brilliant colors. It looked far more inviting than the forest.

"And it is a shortcut to the Land of Freedom," Thomas said aloud. "I'll get home quicker if I go that way."

"You certainly will!" declared a bug that had appeared out of nowhere.

Thomas jumped in surprise. As he turned, the boy was amazed to see a bug that was as tall as he was and dressed in a coat and top hat.

"Where did you come from?" Thomas asked.

"It doesn't matter where you are from or where you are going," the bug replied in a very businesslike tone. "All that matters is if you are having fun."

"Huh?"

The bug looked at the boy impatiently. Waving his cane, he said, "Who cares where you are from? You aren't there anymore! And who cares where you are going? You may never get there! All that matters is where you are and if you're having fun."

Thomas gave the bug a quizzical look. "Well," he finally replied, "I'm traveling to the Land of Freedom."

The bug's eyes widened momentarily. "So you are," he mused. "In that case, you need to take the shortcut. The best way to find freedom is to go to Everything City."

"Everything City?"

"Yes. It's the freest city in all the land."

"The freest?" asked Thomas, his eyes getting wider. The boy had already forgotten the wizard's warning.

"Of course," affirmed the bug as he pointed with his cane toward the city. By now, both he and Thomas had begun walking down the road in that direction.

"In Everything City," the bug continued, "everyone can do everything. It is freedom at its very best."

"Everything?" Thomas asked incredulously.

"Everything," the bug replied firmly. Looking at the boy, he declared, "In Everything City, you can eat all the candy you want."

"Really?"

"And there is no homework," the bug stated flatly. "In Everything City, you only do what you want to do. Everyone is completely free to do whatever they want. Now, that's freedom!"

Thomas' thoughts were still fixed on the idea of eating all of the candy he wanted. Candy sounded fun, but what he really wanted was ice cream – lots and lots of ice cream. He began walking faster toward Everything City. He could hardly wait to get there.

"In Everything City, everyone can do everything."

II

Everything City

As Thomas and the bug approached Everything City, the boy became more and more excited. A wall circled the city, but Thomas could hear all kinds of noise and music coming from inside. It sounded to him like everyone was having a lot of fun! All of the buildings were painted in bright colors and a huge sign just above the entrance read:

Welcome! Do Whatever You Want!

Thomas gazed in awe as they approached the great city. It was almost too much to take in. Two guards opened the city gates as the pair arrived.

Just inside, there stood a short, round man with a prim mustache and fancy coat. He looked to Thomas every bit like a waiter from a very fancy restaurant. He even had a towel over his arm.

"Welcome to Everything City," the waiter bowed.

Thomas bowed back, unsure if he was supposed to or not. The bug looked on impatiently.

"You have arrived at Everything City," announced the bug. "You can eat anything you want and do anything you please. Go and enjoy true freedom."

"Anything I want?" asked Thomas again.

"Yes, anything," affirmed the waiter pleasantly. "What would you like to start with?"

Thomas thought for just a moment. "How about an ice cream sundae?"

"Certainly," declared the waiter. "What would you like on the sundae?"

"I want lots of vanilla ice cream with chocolate sauce and colored sprinkles and whipped cream," Thomas said excitedly, ". . . and a cherry, please."

The waiter bowed and quickly departed. In just a matter of moments, he was back with the sundae.

"Let's explore Everything City as you eat your sundae," suggested the bug, smiling cunningly.

Thomas didn't like the smile, but it did seem like a good suggestion. As they strolled through the city, Thomas saw people having lots of fun and scurrying all about. The bug pointed with his cane to a group of jitterbugs dancing to the music of a small band. The bugs were fascinating to watch as they bounced all over the place.

Thomas continued to eat his sundae as he enjoyed the dancers. Before long, though, he had eaten it all up.

"That's funny," he remarked to the bug. "My sundae is gone and I'm still hungry."

The bug smiled broadly. "Isn't that wonderful?" he said. "Instead of getting an upset stomach when you eat, you are still hungry. Now you can eat an even bigger sundae right away."

Thomas thought about it for just a little while. Another sundae did sound good, and he was still hungry.

"May I have another, please?" he asked the waiter.

The waiter bowed and returned promptly with a second, even larger, sundae which the boy quickly gobbled up. As his spoon clanked in the bottom of the empty sundae dish, though, Thomas still felt hungry.

In fact, Thomas thought he might be even hungrier than before he had devoured the first sundae. He wondered how that could be. The first sundae was large enough that it should have given him an upset stomach. Thomas then wondered, *"If you don't get a stomach ache eating a sundae, do you ever get full?"*

Thomas could also hear his mother's voice in his head, advising him not to eat too many sweets. *"But this isn't home,"* Thomas thought. *"Things are different here."*

After deliberating for a few moments, Thomas said decidedly, "I would like another sundae."

This time, Thomas sat at a table to eat his third sundae. Once finished, he ordered a fourth sundae, and a fifth, and a sixth, eagerly gobbling down each one. As he finished his sixth sundae, however, Thomas realized that he was still hungry. In fact, Thomas was a lot hungrier now than before he had started eating the sundaes.

"I must have another sundae!" he demanded somewhat impolitely. Thomas was finally getting used to the idea that he could have whatever he wanted.

"Coming right up," responded the waiter cheerfully.

In moments, another big sundae appeared in front of Thomas. It was larger than all of the previous ones and had mounds of ice cream, extra cherries and three kinds of syrup dripping down the sides. In addition, it was topped with twice as much whipped cream as before! Eagerly, the boy grabbed his spoon and began to reach for the treat.

"Not so fast," interrupted the bug. He stretched out his cane and blocked Thomas from eating the sundae.

"What do you mean?" Thomas asked indignantly.

"I mean," said the bug sternly, "that you can't have any more sundaes."

Thomas' stomach was aching in hunger. It made him so uncomfortable that he lost his temper.

"That's not true," he said angrily. "This is Everything City. I can do everything I want here."

"That's true," agreed the bug, smiling triumphantly. "You can do everything you want here . . . but you have to pay for it," he added menacingly.

"Pay for it?"

"Yes," declared the bug, pulling out a long roll of paper. "And by my calculations, you owe us 250 gondols."

"250 gondols?"

"Yes," the bug continued in a very businesslike fashion. "Seven ice cream sundaes at 30 gondols each, musical entertainment at 15 gondols, and table and chair rental at 25 gondols. That's 250 gondols."

Thomas sat still, dumbfounded. He had never expected that he would have to pay for what he had eaten.

"I don't think I have any gondols," he finally divulged.

The bug's face beamed happily. "That's perfectly fine," he announced. "You can work to earn some gondols so that you can pay off your debt."

"Work?"

"Why, yes," the bug asserted. "Work. We have lots of coal in the basement that needs to be shoveled."

Thomas frowned. He didn't like the idea of shoveling coal very much. Of course, he had never shoveled coal before. So he told himself that it might not be so bad after all. Besides, Thomas was feeling such strong hunger pains that he was willing to do almost anything to get another sundae.

"Alright," he conceded.

Immediately, the new sundae was pushed in front of him and Thomas ate it as quickly as he could. It tasted so delicious that he gobbled up every last morsel. Once it was gone, the bug informed Thomas that it was time to start shoveling coal.

Shoveling Coal

III

Shoveling Coal

Thomas and the bug clambered down a long flight of stairs to the basement of the city. The boy was surprised to find even more people there below than he had seen above ground. They were all working hard hauling coal.

"Where are they moving the coal to?" he asked.

"Oh," remarked the bug nonchalantly, "They will move it from here to there."

"What happens when it's all moved?"

The bug gave the boy a look of surprise, "Why, they will move it from there to here, of course!"

Thomas frowned. Before he could question the wisdom of this arrangement, however, his stomach began to rumble and he realized how much he was longing for another ice cream sundae. Grabbing a nearby shovel, Thomas selected a pile of coal and started hauling it across the basement. With his aching stomach urging him on, Thomas worked as fast as he could.

After a while, Thomas was feeling exhausted and he decided to take a short rest. He leaned his shovel against the wall and sat down. The bug immediately came over to him and tapped the boy's shovel with his cane.

"You had better keep working," he said sharply.

"How much have I earned so far?" Thomas wondered.

The bug pulled out his paper and began to make some lengthy calculations. Thomas could hear him muttering words like "integral," "square root," and "regression." He wasn't sure if he had ever heard such words before.

Finally, the bug put away his notes and announced with great satisfaction, "Five gondols."

Thomas gasped. "Five gondols? That's all?"

"Don't worry," the bug replied cheerily. "I can let you have a sundae right now and just add it to your bill."

Thomas frowned. If he needed another sundae after only earning five gondols, then he would never earn enough to pay for all he had eaten. But he was so hungry!

"Okay," he conceded.

The bug smiled and presented Thomas with another ice cream sundae. The boy immediately began eating. Soon, the sundae was gone and, to Thomas' dismay, he was still hungry. In fact, he felt as if he hadn't eaten in days!

Thomas thought of asking for another sundae, but then he realized how much it would cost him. Why, he might never get out of this basement! Thomas started to miss his family and he began to cry.

Immediately, the waiter appeared with another sundae. Thomas looked at it longingly and almost took it. Then he reminded himself that it would only make him even hungrier. Thomas was already hungry enough.

"No," he announced to the waiter, shaking his head.

The waiter looked at Thomas with surprise and scurried away. In minutes, the bug reappeared, walking quickly with his cane.

"What's the matter?" he asked brusquely.

"Nothing," replied Thomas.

"I have been told that you don't want to eat any more sundaes. Is that true?"

Thomas gritted his teeth and nodded yes.

"Are you sure?" questioned the bug, waving a delicious sundae in front of the boy. "I'll even let you have this one for free!"

Thomas might have given in if the sundae had not been offered for free. At the mention of the word, the boy realized that nothing in Everything City was truly free. The freedom the bug had promised him wasn't really freedom at all. Everyone in the city was a slave to the bug and always hungry for more of what they wanted. This wasn't freedom!

Strengthened, Thomas replied firmly, "No. I don't want any more sundaes! They aren't free and this isn't freedom! You can keep all of your sundaes."

The bug started to speak, but Thomas ignored him.

Instead, the boy turned around and picked up his shovel. He knew that he had a lot of work to do to pay off his debt. As Thomas labored, the bug and the waiter were busy as well. Soon, they had a table and chair set up in the basement. On the table was the largest sundae Thomas had ever seen! Around it were signs that read:

You Deserve a Break

and

Free Sundae

The boy gazed longingly at the sundae. It had chocolate sauce, sprinkles and twice as many cherries as there had been on any of his other sundaes.

After a few minutes, a band appeared and began to play soft, soothing music. "Come and eat. Eat all you want. Reward yourself. You have worked very hard," sang one of the musicians in an inviting voice.

It was almost more than Thomas could take. Then, he began to think of how much he missed his family. As he did, the power of the sundae and the music became weaker and weaker.

The bug and the waiter frowned. They could see that Thomas wasn't about to have another sundae. Finally, the bug pulled a whistle out of his vest pocket and blew it three times. Immediately, a small troop of soldiers rushed over and snapped to attention.

"I declare this boy's debt paid!" the bug proclaimed. "But there will be no more sundaes for him! Get rid of him right away!"

Immediately, Thomas was picked up by the soldiers. They carried him out of the basement and back through the city. Then, just outside the city gates, the soldiers dumped him on the ground. Thomas watched as the soldiers went back inside and slammed the gates shut behind themselves.

Stumbling to his feet, the boy nearly tripped over his backpack. He glanced inside it and saw that the Lantern of Elsdat was still there. It wasn't broken, but Thomas was surprised to see that the light was very dim, almost out. He breathed a sigh of relief that he hadn't lost it and began to wonder what to do next.

"I guess I should just go back to the road sign," he said to himself out loud.

"Not necessarily," came a voice from behind Thomas. It was the bug again.

Thomas frowned at him.

"I can get permission to let you back into the city," the bug continued. "There's an ice cream festival tonight. Wouldn't a big banana split taste delicious right now?"

As Thomas listened to the bug, he began to feel hungrier and hungrier. But this time, along with the hunger, came fear. Thomas was afraid that his resolve might weaken and he would choose to go back into the city again. If he did, he might never make it to the Land of Freedom!

"No!" the boy shouted. Sticking his fingers in his ears, he ran away from the city and back to the place where he had first met the bug.

"Of course," snapped the tree. *"If you had been raised properly, you would have known that."*

IV

The Forest of Law

As he approached the first signpost once again, Thomas slowed down to catch his breath. It had been a long run back to his starting point.

Thomas dropped to the ground and rested against the signpost. From his seat, the boy's eyes could follow the path to the Land of Freedom as it led into the forest. Even though it had gotten quite hot and sunny, the forest still looked dark and scary.

"*Maybe it's not so bad*," he said to himself. "*Everything City looked fun, but its looks were deceiving.*"

Thomas decided that he couldn't delay his journey much longer. He didn't want to get caught in the forest after dark! The boy began to walk cautiously down the narrow path. At the entrance to the forest, he noticed a sign nailed to a tree. It was a simple white sign with very neat black letters. It read:

> *Welcome to the Forest of Law*
> *Law is Freedom*

"*That's a curious sign,*" he thought.

Thomas entered the forest. The trees were dark green and thick with branches that hung down low. Several times, he had to duck to get past them. To make matters even worse, the path was very narrow and rocky.

After tripping for a third time, Thomas decided to walk beside the path instead of on it. That way, he would be less likely to twist his ankle.

Stepping off to the side, the boy was surprised to hear a stern voice order him, "Get back on the path!"

Thomas jumped back onto the path at once. Frightened, he looked around to see where the voice had come from. There was no one in sight!

Cautiously, Thomas began to make his way forward once more. The voice did not speak again as he picked his way along the rocky path. After tripping a few more times, though, Thomas decided to risk walking beside the path one more time.

Just as before, the instant his foot left the path, a voice boomed, "Get back on the path!"

Thomas jumped back in place once again and tried to find the source of the voice. Before he could, though, a tree reached down with one of its branches and swatted him smartly on the behind.

"Ouch!" he yelped in surprise.

"That was for your own good," the tree replied sternly as it swung its branch back into place.

Thomas stared in amazement at the tree.

"You talk!" he exclaimed.

"As does every other tree in the forest," the tree replied matter-of-factly.

Thomas examined the other trees around him. They all looked to him just like normal trees back home.

"Then why are they so quiet?" he asked.

"Because silence is golden. Haven't you heard that?" the tree scolded him.

"Um, yes," Thomas answered.

"Well, it's true," declared the tree in a sharp voice. "And here in the Forest of Law, we follow the law as perfectly as possible. That's true freedom."

"Really?" asked Thomas.

"Of course," snapped the tree. "If you had been raised properly, you would have known that."

Thomas thought about it for a moment. He had a lot of rules at home, but that didn't feel much like freedom to him. Then, Thomas shuddered as he remembered what had happened to him in Everything City. Maybe the tree was right. Following rules seemed like it might bring better results than simply having everything you wanted.

"Get moving!" the tree ordered.

"W-w-what?" stammered Thomas.

"Get moving! If you stand still, you'll block the way and

that's impolite. So, you need to get moving!" the tree repeated impatiently.

Obediently, Thomas began to stumble down the path.

"And stay on the path!" the tree called after him.

Walking on the path was very difficult, but Thomas did the best he could. After half an hour, he had only been swatted three times by various trees. Still, it felt to him as if he couldn't stop making mistakes.

Finally, the forest opened up slightly and Thomas was relieved to find that he was nearing a small town. It appeared to be a quaint place, with just a few streets and only one section of larger buildings. All of the residents seemed to be going about their business as properly and courteously as possible.

As Thomas entered the town, a short man hurried up and introduced himself.

"Welcome to Lawful Loch Lomen," he said with a deep bow. "I am Mayor Mingle and, as a public servant, I am here to help you."

Thomas stared at the mayor in awe. He was very well-dressed, clean and looked every bit as important as the boy suspected that a mayor should look.

"Well? Aren't you going to say thank you?" the mayor chided Thomas.

"What do you mean?" Thomas asked. The mayor had not really done anything for him, so Thomas was feeling a bit bewildered by his request.

"Well," the mayor said to him very officially, "the right thing to do would have been for you to first say thank you for my offer of assistance. Then, you should have refused my help because you don't want to be a bother to anyone. That's the right thing to do, and here, in Lawful Loch Lomen, we always do the right thing. If you make a mistake like that again, I shall have to send you to jail."

"Jail?" Thomas exclaimed in astonishment.

"Of course," asserted Mayor Mingle. "If you fail to obey the law, the only lawful thing to do is to put you in jail."

"I see," said Thomas, although he wasn't so certain that he really did.

"Well, then," announced the mayor. "As I said, you must be going now. It was good to meet you."

Thomas stared at the mayor for a moment. His head was still spinning from the idea of going to jail for not saying thank you. Finally, he said in his most polite voice, "Thank you for your kind offer, but I don't want to be a bother."

"You're welcome," replied Mayor Mingle, who then turned and walked purposefully away.

Mayor Mingle

V

Lawful Loch Lomen

The mayor departed, leaving Thomas all alone and a bit confused about what he ought to do next. He was quite certain that he couldn't stand still, but Thomas didn't know what else to do. After a moment, he decided to go further into the town.

This time, the walk was very pleasant. Everyone he met smiled and said hello. The men tipped their hats and all the ladies curtsied. Thomas began to think that things might turn out just fine, here in Lawful Loch Lomen.

Suddenly, a voice cried out with great authority, "Stop!"

Thomas was pretty sure that to keep walking would be wrong, so he stopped immediately. Then a large man in uniform strode up to the boy. On the police officer's chest was a badge that identified him as Deputy Dingle.

"I'm sorry," sighed Thomas, who was sure that he had done something wrong, although he had no idea what.

"Ahem," said the deputy as he pulled out a notepad from his shirt pocket. "During your short time here in Lawful

Loch Lomen, I've noticed that you greeted no one 'good day' when they nodded and that you failed to offer any assistance to little old ladies while they plodded."

"But, but . . ." stammered Thomas, who hadn't seen any little old ladies, plodding or otherwise.

"No buts," corrected Deputy Dingle. "Arguing with an officer of the law is against the law. You will find yourself in jail for all of these infractions."

Thomas sighed again. "I'm sorry," he apologized, "but I just arrived and I don't know any of the laws here."

Deputy Dingle puffed himself up. "Ignorance of the law is no excuse. Besides, we have an entire library devoted to the law here in town," he said, gesturing to a marble building just down the street. "Why, if you wanted, you could read all 1,137 volumes at any time."

"1,137 volumes?" Thomas asked incredulously. "How many laws are there?"

"134,587," the deputy replied with great satisfaction.

Thomas shook his head in wonder. "How does anyone keep track of them all?" he asked.

"Why," answered Deputy Dingle, "we go to school, of course. Don't you go to school?"

Not waiting for a reply, the officer continued, "We have school every day, except Sunday, to teach our children the law. They have civil law in the mornings, afternoon classes on criminal law, and lunch sessions on the entire judicial process. On Saturdays, we cover torts."

Torts sounded like tarts to Thomas and that reminded him that he was still very hungry. He wanted to ask Deputy Dingle where he might get some food, but he was afraid he would break a law trying. Finally, his stomach won and Thomas asked, "Excuse me, but is there somewhere I could get some lunch?"

Deputy Dingle looked in horror as everyone within earshot rushed over to offer Thomas some food. Once they had gathered about him, though, no one was willing to speak. They were afraid of being rude to the others. For several moments the entire group stood still, unsure of what to do. Finally, the mayor arrived to investigate.

"Deputy Dingle, what's the cause of this disturbance?" he demanded.

Deputy Dingle began to explain the situation, but once he mentioned Thomas, Mayor Mingle stopped listening. Turning to the boy, the mayor said accusingly, "So, this is all your fault, is it?"

Thomas wanted to answer him, but he could find no safe words to say. Mingle and Dingle stepped aside to confer with each other.

Finally, Mayor Mingle came forward and announced, "This young man is to be arrested and put in jail for inciting a disturbance. You may all disperse now."

Thomas stood dumbfounded as the people departed. He never imagined he could get in trouble just for asking where to get some lunch. In short order, though, Deputy Dingle grabbed Thomas by the arm and escorted him to the town jail.

The jail wasn't as impressive as Thomas had expected. It was a small wooden building with a porch and a single entrance. Inside, there was a tiny waiting room with three doors leading to three separate cells.

Deputy Dingle opened one of the doors and motioned to the boy to step inside. Thomas shuffled forlornly into his cell and plopped down on the single chair beside the bed. He put his face in his hands and felt like he was about to start crying.

"What am I going to do now?" the boy mourned. *"How will I ever get to the Land of Freedom?"*

Suddenly, Thomas was startled by a voice in the cell.

"Whatcha in for?" the voice asked.

"I wish I knew," Thomas replied sadly, still unsure of where the voice was coming from.

Then, out of the corner of his eye, Thomas noticed a boy about his age sitting on the floor against the wall.

"Who are you?" Thomas asked as he lifted his head up.

"I'm Jimmy," the boy replied. "What's your name?"

"Thomas," Thomas answered as properly as he could.

"It's good to meet you, Thomas," Jimmy replied.

Thomas looked this curious boy over. Jimmy wore a white shirt, plaid shorts held up by suspenders, and a pointed hat. The hat was too small for his head, so the boy's red hair stuck out on both sides. Jimmy looked a bit funny, but he seemed to be a fairly nice boy.

"Why are you in here?" Thomas asked.

"Because I like the freedom."

"What?" asked Thomas. He was quite startled by the boy's answer. What was free about being in a jail cell?

"This is the freest place in town," the boy continued. "I've lived in Lawful Loch Lomen all of my life, and there is no place I would rather be than right here."

Perplexed, Thomas asked him, "Why is that?"

"Isn't it great being in this jail?" Jimmy asked.

VI

Jimmy in Jail

Jimmy laughed and pulled a small toy out of his pocket.

"First," he insisted, "let's play ball."

"Okay," Thomas answered. He was glad to finally do something fun.

The two boys decided to bounce the ball to each other using as many walls as possible. Jimmy sent the ball bouncing off three walls before it landed at Thomas' feet. When Thomas tried, he kept hitting the ceiling, which was, of course, out of bounds.

After a few minutes, Thomas suggested that they keep score. Eventually, when Jimmy had won by 21 points to 17 points, the boys sat down to rest.

It was then that Thomas noticed a tray of food sitting by the door to the cell.

"Is that for us?" he asked.

"Sure," said Jimmy. "Eat all you want. I don't want to have any. I'm full."

By now, Thomas felt like he was about to starve. He hadn't had anything to eat since the ice cream sundaes in Everything City. Thomas quickly ate everything on the tray. The lunch was delicious!

"Isn't it great being in this jail?" Jimmy asked after Thomas had finished eating.

Thomas frowned, "No. Not really."

"Well," said Jimmy as he motioned toward the town. "Being in here is a lot better than being out there. There is no freedom in Lawful Loch Lomen at all."

"What do you mean?" asked Thomas.

"In the town, there are so many laws to follow that you can never do anything you want to do."

Thomas considered this for a moment and decided that Jimmy was probably right. After all, there were 134,587 laws just waiting to be broken by someone.

"Did you know," Jimmy continued, "that we broke five laws in just the past ten minutes?"

"I don't believe you!" Thomas replied.

Jimmy smiled smugly. "Children should be seen and not heard; No roughhousing indoors; Don't mark up the walls; Beds are for sleeping, not jumping on; and If you can't say something nice, then don't say anything at all."

"We broke all of those?"

"Yes," replied Jimmy proudly. "Why, I break about 87 laws a day, not counting duplicates."

"Oh my," was all Thomas could think to say. "How long will you be in jail?"

Jimmy paused and then answered, "I'll be in here for another 434 years, 11 months, 7 days and 3 hours."

"Doesn't that make you sad?"

"Not really," claimed Jimmy. "Out there, you can go anywhere you want, but you can't do anything. In here, I may not be able to go anywhere, but I can do whatever I want."

Thomas didn't think that either situation sounded very much like freedom, but he decided not to say anything. A few minutes later, Thomas and Jimmy heard the clanking of keys as the mayor and the police officer arrived outside the jail cell.

"Well, young man," Mayor Mingle said once the cell door was opened, "have you learned your lesson?"

"I think so . . . maybe," Thomas answered hesitantly, unsure of what lesson he was supposed to have learned.

"Good!" proclaimed the mayor, smiling broadly in a very official way.

Thomas thought it might be best to stay quiet again, but he couldn't help himself.

"Mister Mayor?" he asked.

"Yes?"

"The sign outside the forest says that law is freedom. What does that mean?"

Mayor Mingle puffed himself up to his full stature and replied, "It's simple, my boy. Without rules, people do things that are wrong. They hurt themselves and each other. When that happens, no one is happy. Rules, on the other hand, keep us from doing wrong and hurting others. You see, true freedom is when you are free to do what's right, not free to do what's wrong."

Mayor Mingle smiled at Thomas with great satisfaction, but the boy wasn't sure if he agreed. Freedom that told you what to do all the time didn't sound much like freedom to him. Maybe Jimmy was right. Maybe he was freer in jail than the people who were out of jail.

"Ahem," said Deputy Dingle very officially. "You have been charged with inciting a disturbance. The penalty for your crime, as a first time offender and taking into account your youth, is three days, not including time served, of course."

"Three days?" Thomas exclaimed. "That's a long time!"

"Yes," replied the mayor, "but it's for your own good."

Just then, Deputy Dingle peeked inside the cell. "Oh, no!" he said with alarm. "The boys have been playing in the cell. They've marked up the walls!"

Mayor Mingle also looked inside the cell. He came back out with a worried expression on his face. "The penalty for roughhousing indoors is four days in jail. Add to that five more days for marking up the walls, one day for jumping on the bed and two days for being not just seen, but also heard. Young man, you will have to remain in jail for fifteen more days," the mayor announced.

Fifteen more days! Thomas groaned. This was worse than being in Everything City! With 134,587 laws that he could break, Thomas might not ever get out of jail! And even if he did, he was sure to be thrown back in before he could get out of town. It was hopeless!

As he thought of having to spend the rest of his life locked up in jail, the boy started to sob. Mayor Mingle and Deputy Dingle looked on sympathetically, but they didn't offer any help. Then Thomas began to get angry. All of these laws! They didn't make people any happier than having no laws at all! Lawful Loch Lomen, he decided, was just as bad as Everything City!

Suddenly, Thomas had an idea. If there were 134,587 laws, certainly there had to be one or two about how to treat guests. Wiping his tears away, the boy stood up to the two officials.

"Whatever happened to following the law about being kind to strangers?" he demanded.

Mingle and Dingle recoiled in shock.

"Or what about the laws to treat others with respect or to consider other people's needs ahead of your own?" Thomas continued angrily.

Both the mayor and the police officer took another step back from the boy.

"I think that you both should be here in jail with me!" Thomas shouted.

"Careful!" Mayor Mingle cautioned nervously. "You are about to incite a disturbance again."

The Supreme Court

VII

The Supreme Court

Mayor Mingle and Deputy Dingle stepped aside to talk for a moment. Finally, the mayor turned back toward Thomas and said, "Your case is a very serious one, and it is clear to us that you have not learned your lesson. We must go before the Supreme Court."

In a matter of minutes, Thomas found himself being escorted down the street by the deputy and the mayor to the Supreme Court. People on every side stepped out of the way and murmured hopeful things to him, just as the law required.

The Supreme Court building had many tall columns and a number of stairs. After going up all 38 of them, the small party entered the courthouse. Inside was a large lobby with four massive doors at the far end. They were at least twenty feet high and looked very imposing.

As Thomas and his escorts approached, two doormen dressed in long, black coats with silver epaulets gravely directed them into the courtroom. Once inside, Thomas heard the doors close behind him with an ominous thud.

The courtroom was as solemn and stately as any place Thomas could ever imagine. There were a number of people in the room, all quietly going about their work. Still, every noise, no matter how slight, seemed to echo endlessly off the marble floor and walls.

In the front of the room, a row of chairs was placed behind a long, raised table. It seemed to Thomas that the judges probably sat there. The scene was so formal that he was afraid to speak. After a moment, the boy was directed to sit down. Thomas sat quietly, wondering how many laws he had broken since leaving the jail.

A minute later, the bailiff, a short man who wore a great powdered wig announced, "All rise for the Supreme Court! Court is now in session!"

Seven judges entered the courtroom and took their seats behind the long table. Each one wore a black robe and a wig just like the bailiff's. None of them smiled or even acknowledged Thomas in any way. He had never seen such a serious gathering in all his life. It reminded Thomas of the time when he and his friend, John, had gotten in trouble at school and his parents had to meet with his teacher, Mrs. Warden.

"Be seated!" announced the bailiff in a very official tone of voice.

Thomas sat down as quickly and obediently as he could.

"Ahem!" said the judge who was seated in the middle of the seven justices. "In the case of the People of Lawful Loch Lomen versus Young Master Thomas, Thomas is accused of breaking the following laws:"

"Inciting a disturbance"

"Roughhousing indoors"

"Marking up the walls"

"Jumping on the bed"

"Being not just seen but also heard"

"Does the prosecutor have any further comments?"

A tall, skinny man with wiry gray hair and thin, round spectacles rose from the table across the aisle from Thomas.

"Your Honor," he began, "I am Prosecutor Pingle. It is indeed a privilege to represent the people of Lawful Loch Lomen before this Supreme Court."

The chief justice nodded his head, acknowledging the prosecutor's words, which, by the way, were required by law under statue C-174, section B, paragraph five.

"Are there any additional comments for the court?"

"No, your Honor," replied Prosecutor Pingle.

The chief justice looked down sternly at Thomas, who was already quite afraid. "Young man, do you have any remarks?" he asked.

Thomas sat still, too afraid to say or do anything.

"Well?" asked the chief justice again.

This time, Thomas decided that he needed to speak up. He figured that maybe what he had said in the jail might work again. Nervously, the boy stood to his feet.

"Yes, your Majesty, um, I mean, your Honor," he began. "I came here not knowing any of the laws and I haven't been treated very kindly. I'm sure that the mayor and the police officer have broken several laws about how to treat strangers and about being kind to others."

Thomas stood still, his knees shaking, as everyone in the room stared in disbelief. To speak against a person in a position of authority was a serious violation of the law! Everyone knew that!

The chief justice glared down at Thomas with great concern. Being locked up with Jimmy should have taught the boy to be obedient, but apparently it had not. It appeared to the judge that Thomas might never be willing to follow the law.

The chief justice stood up, followed by the remaining justices. The bailiff quickly scrambled to his feet and called out, "All rise!"

"There will be a short recess before the verdict," stated the chief justice. He and the other judges filed out of the courtroom, their robes flowing behind them.

Thomas sat down. He was tired and sad. How would he ever get out of this mess? Glancing at his backpack, he saw that the Lantern of Elsdat was still there. It was once again shining very dimly.

Meanwhile, Mingle, Dingle and Pingle all whispered quietly together. They had never seen the court take a recess before rendering a decision. Usually, the answer was plain for everyone to see. If not, they would simply announce a new law that explained what should be done.

Thomas overhead the mayor saying to the other two, "This is, indeed, a unique situation."

Finally, after a very uncomfortable half hour in which Thomas broke at least three more laws, the justices returned to the courtroom.

"Hear ye! Hear ye!" announced the bailiff in his most official sounding voice.

"The Supreme Court of Lawful Loch Lomen is now in session. All rise for the reading of the verdict."

Everyone in the room stood to their feet. Then, as the chief justice looked very sternly at Thomas, the bailiff read the court's decision.

"The Supreme Court renders its decision today in great seriousness," he began. "We have before us a young man who refuses to follow the law and is disturbing all of Lawful Loch Lomen. He has done this even though he was fully aware that he could be imprisoned for the rest of his life."

"Therefore," the bailiff continued, "in the case of the People of Lawful Loch Lomen versus Young Master Thomas, it is the decision of the Supreme Court to impose the greatest punishment possible."

There was an audible gasp in the courtroom.

"Silence!" declared the bailiff.

Everyone stared at the boy with alternating faces of horror, sympathy and righteous condemnation, all of which were, of course, required by the law.

Thomas squirmed in his shoes, wondering what this greatest possible punishment could be. Would he be sent back to jail for life with Jimmy?

The bailiff concluded, "It is the judgment of this court that Master Thomas be banished from the town of Lawful Loch Lomen immediately and never allowed to return. In losing all laws, he is losing all freedom."

This time, a low murmur by the audience could be heard in the courtroom.

"Silence!" ordered the bailiff again. "Remain standing for the departure of the Supreme Court!"

The seven judges rose from their seats and proceeded out of the courtroom in single file. As they were departing, Thomas began to realize that he was going to get to leave Lawful Loch Lomen! A smile started to light up his face, but he quickly stifled it. Thomas didn't want to do anything that might cause the justices to change their minds.

Once the judges had left and the hearing concluded, Mingle, Dingle and Pingle all came over to Thomas.

"Very sad outcome," consoled Mayor Mingle.

"So sorry," added Deputy Dingle.

"My condolences," Prosecutor Pingle chimed in.

"Be that as it may," said Mayor Mingle, assuming a very official posture. "It is now our solemn duty to carry out the orders of the court. Deputy Dingle, please escort Master Thomas out of town and send him into exile."

It seemed to Thomas that there was a slight note of disappointment in the mayor's voice. He guessed that Mayor Mingle would have been secretly quite happy to keep Thomas in jail for the rest of his life.

The boy quickly grabbed his backpack and followed the deputy as obediently as possible. Once outside, he made certain to greet everyone good day, whether they nodded or not. He also kept a sharp eye out for any plodding old ladies so that he could assist them.

It didn't take long to get to the edge of town since Lawful Loch Lomen wasn't very big.

"Ahem," said Deputy Dingle with all formality. "It is the decision of the Supreme Court of Lawful Loch Lomen to banish you forever. You are to leave by this path and never return again."

The deputy turned abruptly and walked away, leaving Thomas standing alone. The path in front of him led into the forest on the opposite side of the town from where he had arrived. For Thomas, that meant that he could only go forward. There was no way to return to where he had previously been.

Thaddeus Thudge

VIII

The Ladder of Success

Thomas stood still for just a moment before realizing that he might be doing something wrong. He was, after all, still in the Forest of Law. Quickly, the boy picked up his backpack. As he put it on, he noticed that the Lantern of Elsdat was burning more brightly than before.

In minutes, Thomas was walking briskly down the narrow path through the Forest of Law. The path wasn't as rocky on this side of the village, so he made better time than before.

Every now and then, a tree would yell at him or try to swat him with its branches. He was used to them by now, so their rebukes didn't bother Thomas that much. After an hour's hike, the forest began to thin out and a beautiful meadow came into view.

With a sigh of relief, Thomas stepped out of the forest and into the meadow. Almost at once, the narrow path turned into a small road. It was getting darker now, so the boy decided to find a comfortable place where he could settle down for the night.

The next morning, Thomas was awakened by the warm sunshine on his face. It felt good. Once he had gotten up, the boy continued his journey along the road through the meadow. In just a few minutes he arrived at a fork in the road. There, Thomas found another signpost with two, small, hand-lettered signs. One pointed to the left and read:

Land of Freedom

The sign beneath it pointed to the right and read:

Success

Thomas knew he needed to go to the left, but he paused for a moment to examine the road to success. Just down the street stood a very fancy house, one of the grandest Thomas had ever seen. As he marveled at it, Thomas found himself inching down the road to get a closer look. Soon, he was standing right in front of the house.

"Isn't it a beautiful place?" inquired a portly man who came strolling down the driveway.

"*It certainly is*," thought Thomas to himself. "*This house is lots better than ours.*"

"I am Thaddeus Thudge," the man continued, extending his hand, "I'm the most successful man in the world."

"Thomas," the boy introduced himself and shook Mr. Thudge's hand. "Is that your house?"

"Why, yes. Do you want to take a look inside?"

Thomas paused, remembering what his parents had said about going places with strangers. "*But everyone here is a stranger*," Thomas told himself. So, forgetting for the moment about his journey to the Land of Freedom, he agreed to go inside.

Soon, Thomas and his host were touring Thaddeus' mansion. The boy marveled at how all of the rooms were filled with beautiful furniture and extravagantly decorated. He was even more amazed, though, when he saw the game room. Every game that Thomas had ever heard of seemed to be there, as well as bins of toys stacked against the walls. There was even a butler present to clean up any messes.

"Do you like knives?" asked Mr. Thudge. He had seen Thomas looking at a knife collection in a display case. "You may have one if you like."

"Really?"

"Yes, of course. I can get more whenever I want. Here, have this pocketknife. It's the best one in the display."

"Thank you!" Thomas said, remembering his manners.

Happily, the boy stuffed the knife into his pants pocket and continued the tour. As they walked outside, he saw a basketball court, a big swimming pool, a miniature golf course, an archery range and a huge playground.

"How did you get all of this?" Thomas asked.

Thaddeus smiled broadly, "Just as I said. I'm the most successful man in the world. I bought all of this and I could buy a lot more if I wanted."

"Say," the man continued, "you look a bit hungry to me. Would you like some food?"

Thomas thought twice about the offer. He could still remember what had happened to him in Everything City. But he was hungry and he did need to eat.

"Yes, please," the boy answered.

Thaddeus snapped his fingers. Moments later, several servants brought in a lunch of chili and hot dogs, two of Thomas' favorite foods. He gobbled them down quickly, trying to be polite even though he was hungry. Finally, the boy finished. He was full and it felt good.

"How would you like to live in a mansion as big as this one?" Thaddeus asked.

"*Oh, boy!*" thought Thomas to himself. "Of course I would!" he replied.

"I can show you how," said the man.

The eager look on Thomas' face was the only answer Thaddeus needed. They went back through the game room and down a long hallway that was lined with many doors. Each door had a sign on it. Finally, they stopped in front of a door labeled:

Ladder of Success #121

Mr. Thudge pulled a key out from his pocket and opened the door. The small room had no windows, no furniture, and no other doors. Instead, in the middle of the room there was a ladder that stretched from the floor way up past where the ceiling should have been.

As Thomas looked up, he marveled to see that the ladder went straight up and out of sight.

"What is this?" he asked.

"This is the ladder of success," Mr. Thudge answered. "If you want to be as successful as me, all you need to do is climb this ladder all the way to the top. Once you do, you will be successful."

"Not only that," Thaddeus continued knowingly, "once you are successful, you will have complete freedom."

Thomas looked doubtfully at the ladder of success. It seemed very high. It looked like a difficult climb all the way to the top.

"Go up a few steps and see what it's like."

Thomas thought for a moment. Didn't his teacher say that he should be willing to try new things? His mom always said so at dinner. Grabbing the ladder, Thomas began to climb. He was surprised at how fast it was. In just a few seconds, he was already ten feet high.

"Wow!" he exclaimed. "This is easy!"

Thaddeus beamed. "Yes, isn't it? You will reach the top of the ladder of success in no time."

Thomas thought for just a moment. The game room was so exciting! Maybe the sign outside was wrong. The ladder of success might really be the way to the Land of Freedom. After all, if Thomas could reach success, then surely he would be free.

Turning to Mr. Thudge, Thomas declared, "I will climb to the top of the ladder of success!"

*When Thomas had started,
the climb was rapid and easy.*

IX

Climbing the Ladder

"Very good!" congratulated Mr. Thudge, rubbing his hands together in delight. "You are going to be an excellent climber, my boy!"

Thaddeus paused, "I think I have some other guests coming. You get climbing and I'll be back in a short while to see how you are doing."

Thomas didn't even bother to watch Thaddeus leave. Instead, he began climbing as fast as he could. Soon, the air around him grew foggy, but that was no concern to Thomas. He was making great progress. Thomas was sure that he wasn't very far from the top.

After climbing for quite some time, though, he began to notice that he wasn't moving as quickly as before. When Thomas had started, the climb was rapid and easy. Now, it took a lot of effort just to lift one foot up to the next rung. Still, Thomas was pressed on.

Despite his best efforts, Thomas soon found that he was barely making any progress at all. It took almost a full minute of hard work to raise even one foot up to the next rung on the ladder. At this rate, he was afraid that it would take forever to reach the top. In addition, Thomas was becoming quite tired. He even considered climbing back down the ladder.

"*But I've already come so far!*" he said to himself. The boy gritted his teeth and began to lift his foot up to the next rung on the ladder.

After struggling for a long time, Thomas had only made it up two more rungs. As he rested, he almost decided that climbing to the top of the ladder of success was hopeless. But then Thomas reminded himself that Mr. Thudge had done it. If someone like Mr. Thudge could make it to the top, then certainly Thomas could.

Wearily, he began climbing once again, but Thomas barely made any progress at all. He began to wonder how someone the size of Mr. Thudge could have ever accomplished the climb in the first place.

"That's it!" Thomas declared out loud. He would climb down the ladder and ask Mr. Thudge how he made it to the top. Then, Thomas would just do the same thing. Newly energized, the boy began his climb down.

Much to his surprise, the climb down the ladder of success was a lot faster than the climb up. In just a few minutes, Thomas was already at the bottom again. He stood in amazement, looking back up the ladder.

"*I can't believe I got down so quickly!*" the boy said to himself.

Thaddeus wasn't in the room, so Thomas decided to go look for him in the mansion. As he walked to the door, however, Thomas noticed a small sign painted on it that he hadn't seen before. In very neat, red letters, it read:

No Exit

Ignoring the sign, Thomas reached for the door handle, only to discover that there wasn't one. On top of that, the door was locked shut. Thomas was trapped!

Although it wasn't polite, the boy began to pound on the door for help. It was alright, he thought, especially since it was also not polite to lock someone in a room.

After a few minutes of pounding, Thomas felt the door open and Mr. Thudge walked in. His wide frame filled the doorway. He had a pleasant look on his face, but his eyes seemed a bit sinister.

"Yes?" he asked with a note of impatience.

By now, Thomas wasn't interested in getting to the top of the ladder anymore. It seemed to him that he ought to continue his trip as quickly as possible.

"I would like to leave now," he stated. "I don't want to climb the ladder of success anymore."

"Really?" Thaddeus replied. "Well, rest assured young man, you may leave anytime you want."

Thomas started toward the door, but Mr. Thudge kicked it shut with his foot before the boy could get out.

"You did read the sign, though, didn't you?" he said. "You can't leave through that door."

"Then how do I get out of here?"

"The only way out is to climb to the top of the ladder."

Thomas sighed. He didn't want to climb the ladder, but he was glad to know that there was a way out.

"That's a very hard climb," Thomas said to Mr. Thudge. "How did you make it to the top?"

Thaddeus looked around a bit uncomfortably and said, "Shouldn't you get climbing now if you want to leave?"

"First, I need to know how you made it to the top. That way, I can do the same thing," answered Thomas.

Mr. Thudge's face changed and he smiled coldly at the boy. "I never did," he finally answered.

"You never made it to the top of the ladder?"

"No."

"Then, how did you become the most successful man in the world?" Thomas asked in surprise.

Thaddeus smiled and replied, "I became successful by having other people climb for me."

Thomas stared at the man in disbelief.

"Yes," Mr. Thudge continued. "I found these ladders years ago and began to enlist others to climb them for me. There are 150 ladders total and as long as I have enough people climbing them, I stay successful."

"You, my friend," he continued, "cannot leave by going out this door, but if you make it to the top of the ladder, you will be able to leave a success."

Thomas remembered how difficult it was to climb the ladder. "Has anyone ever made it to the top?" he asked.

Mr. Thudge remained uncomfortably silent.

"Well?" asked Thomas again.

"You'd better get climbing if you are going to succeed," replied Thaddeus.

"Not until I have an answer," Thomas insisted. "Has anyone ever made it to the top?"

"Not yet. But I have great expectations that you will be the first," the man said encouragingly. "You are young and strong. I'll wager that you will get to the top of the ladder of success faster than anyone ever thought was possible!"

Thomas thought again about the ladder and the game room. It would be great to be a success, he concluded, but he just knew that Mr. Thudge was lying. No one had ever made it to the top and no one ever would.

In a flash, Thomas knew what he had to do.

The boy ran over to the door a second time. Mr. Thudge stepped aside and smiled. He had seen this many times before. The person would struggle to pry open the door, but as long as Thaddeus had the key, there was no way anyone could get out.

Mr. Thudge's smile disappeared, though, when he saw that Thomas didn't try to force the door open. Instead the boy pulled out his new pocketknife and stuck the blade of the knife deep into the lock.

"Give me the key to this room," Thomas declared, "or I'll break my knife off in the lock and trap you in here forever!"

Mr. Thudge's face grew pale at the thought.

"You wouldn't do that!" he declared.

The man began to approach Thomas, but the boy yelled, "Get back or you'll be trapped in here forever!"

"But you would be trapped as well," Thaddeus argued.

"I am anyway!" Thomas countered, bending his knife in the key hole and staring resolutely at Mr. Thudge.

"Back up and toss me the key!" Thomas ordered.

Thaddeus took several steps back and reached for his key. "Here," he said, his hands shaking. "Here it is."

Thaddeus tossed the key over to Thomas.

Thomas caught the key in midair. Then, pulling the pocketknife out of the lock, he threw it at Mr. Thudge.

"Here! Catch this!" he called.

While Mr. Thudge ducked to avoid being hit by the knife, Thomas quickly unlocked the door. Thaddeus tried to grab the boy, but he was too slow. Thomas bolted out of the room and slammed the door shut behind him, trapping Mr. Thudge inside.

Thomas could hear Thaddeus Thudge's muffled screams as the boy raced quickly through the game room and out of the mansion. Soon, Thomas was back on the road and running to the fork where he had made his wrong turn.

As he thought of the game room again, Thomas felt a tinge of shame that he could have been so greedy. But now, he no longer wanted any of the things that that Mr. Thudge possessed.

Thomas stopped and turned so that he was looking down the road toward Mr. Thudge's mansion. It still looked very beautiful, but now Thomas understood how evil it was. The boy opened his fist and looked at the key he had taken from Mr. Thudge. It was labeled:

Dungeon Room #121

Thomas drew his arm back and, with all of his might, threw the key back down the road as far as he could.

Walking back to the fork in the road, Thomas thought about what it meant to be free. He decided that the ladder of success didn't bring a person freedom. And what kind of freedom was it, anyway, if it depended on trapping other people in slavery?

Helmud the Hudlunk

X

Helmud and the Woods of Woe

This time, when Thomas reached the fork in the road, he was determined to go straight to the Land of Freedom. The road took him along the edge of the woods for the rest of the morning. It was a long walk in the hot sun.

Finally, Thomas decided to sit down and rest for a little while. He checked to see if any of the trees nearby would mind. Hearing no replies, the boy settled down in the shade with his back against a tree.

As he rested, Thomas opened his backpack and pulled out the Lantern of Elsdat. It was shining nicely – not very brightly, but not as dimly as before, either. The boy admired the light for a little while before tucking it back beside his jacket so he could start walking again.

Just as he was getting up to leave, Thomas was startled by a fierce roar coming from the woods behind him. A second roar was even nearer than the first. The boy looked frantically about and then quickly climbed up the closest tree. As he crouched on a branch, Thomas hoped that the approaching creature did not climb trees, too.

The animal's roar grew louder and louder and louder. Soon, Thomas could see the bushes rustling as it approached. He clung to his tree branch in great fright.

Moments later, a big beast with a lion-like head and the muscular body of a huge bulldog leaped out and stood right below him. It was as tall as Thomas and uglier and more terrifying than any animal he had ever seen!

The beast didn't see Thomas, but it had so frightened him that the boy tried frantically to climb higher up the tree. Thomas placed his weight on a slender branch and, in the next instant, there was a loud crack as the bough snapped in two. Legs and arms flailing, the boy fell to the ground directly in front of the ferocious lion-dog.

Cringing in fear, Thomas covered his ears and closed his eyes tight, certain that he was about to be eaten alive. For a few awful moments, he waited, not daring to move a muscle. Then, when nothing happened and no teeth had begun to gnaw on him, Thomas cautiously opened his eyes again.

The strange animal sat there, looking at Thomas. To his amazement, it didn't seem fierce or hungry. Its lion-like head still seemed very scary. But as Thomas looked closer, he saw big tears in the animal's eyes.

Suddenly, the lion-dog roared again. It was such a terrifying sound that Thomas cowered on the ground once more. After a moment, the boy dared to take another look at the beast. This time, he saw even more tears in the animal's eyes. Thomas realized that the beast wasn't angry or ferocious at all. It was sad.

Thomas and the Lantern

"What's the matter?" Thomas asked cautiously.

The lion-dog sniffled and looked curiously at the boy.

"You aren't going to run away, too, are you?" it asked in a deep, rough voice.

"Why, no," said Thomas, even though he understood completely why someone would run away. This animal was scary even when it tried to be friendly.

"What's your name?" he asked.

"I'm Helmud the hudlunk," the creature replied.

Thomas decided that Helmud was a boy hudlunk who was probably not much older than he was.

"I'm Thomas," he said, introducing himself.

"It's good to meet you," sniffed Helmud.

"It's good to meet you, too," Thomas said. He really wasn't all that happy to meet the animal. But it was better, he thought, to have a hudlunk meeting him than it was to have a hudlunk eating him.

"What's the matter?" Thomas asked again.

This time, Helmud looked forlornly at Thomas and he began to explain his woes. "I'm lost and alone," the hudlunk stated. "My parents went out looking for food several days ago and they haven't come back. I'm afraid that a hunter killed them."

"Do you have any friends or other family to be with?" Thomas asked.

The hudlunk burst into tears. He explained that there were no other hudlunks who lived anywhere nearby, and no one ever wanted to be his friend. Thomas could see why, although he didn't tell Helmud that.

Helmud continued to cry, "I'm all alone here in the Woods of Woe."

Thomas sat with the poor creature for quite some time. He had little advice to give, but he could at least listen. After a while, though, Thomas told the hudlunk that he must be going.

"Where are you going?" asked Helmud.

"To the Land of Freedom," Thomas replied.

The hudlunk looked very frightened. "You shouldn't go there," Helmud said.

"I don't have a choice. I have to go there because the wizard commanded me," Thomas explained. He then told the hudlunk how the wizard had appeared in his bedroom and about all of his adventures so far.

"You still shouldn't go," Helmud insisted. "You'll never be able to make it there anyway."

"Why not?"

"Because it's a very long and dangerous journey," the hudlunk said. "It's better if you just stay here in the Woods of Woe with me. We can be sad together."

Thomas shook his head. "My only hope to see my family again is to get to the Land of Freedom. Goodbye, Helmud. I hope you find your family, too."

Helmud watched mournfully as the boy left for the Land of Freedom. Thomas felt sorry for the hudlunk, but he didn't think that the Woods of Woe was a good place to stay for very long. He really did hope that Helmud would find his parents soon. Of course, Thomas also hoped the same thing for himself.

The road continued along beside the woods. It was a bit dusty, but very pleasant to walk on. The gentle breeze made it all the better.

After Thomas had walked for a few minutes, he was surprised when a deep voice called out from behind him, "Thomas! Thomas! Wait for me!"

He turned just in time to see Helmud bounding right up beside him.

"May I come along, too?" the hudlunk asked as he gasped for air.

Thomas looked at the creature in surprise. "Didn't you just say that the land of Freedom was too far away and that the journey was too dangerous?"

Helmud lowered his head.

"Can I come anyway?" he pleaded.

Somehow, Thomas understood that for Helmud, being left all alone was worse than taking a long trip through scary places. He felt sorry for the hudlunk.

"You can come," Thomas decided, "but you can't roar so ferociously."

"Okay," Helmud agreed happily. "Let's go."

Mr. Smith

XI

Ball & Chain

The boy and the hudlunk followed the dirt road in the bright sunshine. As they stayed outside the Woods of Woe, Helmud seemed to get a bit happier. For the first time, Thomas also began to enjoy the journey. Now that there were two of them, the adventure was starting to be more fun.

After a few hours, Thomas noticed a change in the road. Along with finding the footprints of other travelers, he also began to see smooth indentations that were worn into the road's surface. It looked as if someone had been dragging something heavy down the road, but Thomas couldn't imagine what it might be. Helmud did not seem to know what it was, either. He had never traveled this far from home before.

Finally, as they came around a bend in the road, the two companions found the source of the strange markings. There, in front of them, stood a man with a ball and chain connected to his ankle.

"Hi!" the man greeted them cheerfully.

"Hello," Thomas replied. Helmud made no sound, but nodded awkwardly, not wanting to growl and scare the man off.

"I'm Thomas."

"I'm Mr. Smith, S.S. Smith."

The man handed Thomas a business card. It read:

S.S. (Super Sensitive) Smith
Solicitor

Thomas didn't know what to do. The man seemed nice enough, but the ball and chain he wore was very odd. Not only that, but Mr. Smith ignored Thomas' stares and never acknowledged that he even had a ball and chain.

The man started walking with Thomas and Helmud, dragging the ball behind him as he went.

Thomas, of course, felt obliged to make some small talk. So he asked, "Where are we?"

"Where are we?" Mr. Smith responded incredulously. "Well, we are almost at the beautiful City of Bitterness."

"Bitterness?" repeated Thomas.

"Oh, yes. It's the most wonderful city there is. Watch as we come over this rise. You will see the castle in the valley below."

The man then pointed to a very large stone building rising out of a walled city at the end of the valley. It had tall, narrow spires and huge windows with a bright metallic sheen. It was dazzling.

"Whose castle is that?" Thomas wondered aloud.

"It's the home of Queen Juliana, the ruler of the City of Bitterness. That's where I'm going. Are you going there, too?" Mr. Smith asked.

"No. We are headed to the Land of Freedom," Thomas replied cautiously, half expecting a negative response.

"There's no freedom there," Mr. Smith stated flatly.

"No?"

"None. In the Land of Freedom they take everything away from you and make you pretend that you are free."

Thomas was puzzled. "Really?"

"Yes," said Mr. Smith.

By now they had arrived at the entrance to the walled city. It was bursting with activity. Oddly enough, every person Thomas saw had a ball and chain just like Mr. Smith. Some of the balls were quite small and others were very large indeed.

Because the gates to the city were narrow, Thomas realized that some of the people were trapped inside. The ball chained to them was simply too big to pass through the gates.

"You really ought to visit our city," Mr. Smith urged.

Thomas remembered how his visits to Everything City, Lawful Loch Lomen and Mr. Thudge's mansion had all turned out poorly. So he decided to decline the offer. As he did, however, Mr. Smith began to act very offended.

The boy struggled to find a polite way to say that he had to be going, but he couldn't find any words that would soothe Mr. Smith. In addition, each time Mr. Smith got more offended, his ball and chain grew just a bit bigger. Finally, Thomas relented and agreed to visit the city.

"Splendid!" Mr. Smith cried out. "I'll even arrange for you to meet Queen Juliana."

As they entered the city gates, Helmud whispered to Thomas, "Did you see his ball and chain grow?"

The boy nodded.

"Are you two talking about me behind my back?" Mr. Smith asked accusingly.

"No," said Thomas quickly. Afterward he felt guilty, but he told himself that they were really talking about the ball and chain, not Mr. Smith.

As it was, Thomas and Helmud noticed that Mr. Smith's ball seemed to grow a bit larger. The pair followed their host through the streets of the City of Bitterness.

"*Mr. Smith is right,*" Thomas thought to himself. "*This is a beautiful city!*"

Still, he couldn't understand why everyone had a ball and chain, and he was afraid to ask. After walking a few blocks further, the trio approached a guardhouse. It had a sentry wearing a big fluffy hat standing out front.

"This is the entrance to the throne room," Mr. Smith whispered. Addressing the guard, he said, "I have two important visitors for the queen. Show us in right now!"

The sentry eyed Thomas and Helmud closely and then remarked, "They don't look very important to me."

Mr. Smith's face got red and his ball grew larger. "They are very important visitors, actually," he fumed. "If you were a well-trained sentry, you would have realized that right away."

Now, it was the sentry's turn to get angry. He and Mr. Smith began arguing with each other. Thomas' eyes widened as the sentry's ball grew larger as a result. He was afraid the two men would get into a fistfight if this kept up.

"Excuse me," Thomas interrupted. "Maybe if the sentry knew why we were so important, he would allow us to see the queen."

"Yes," accepted the sentry, calming down.

"I agree, too," said Mr. Smith, although he didn't seem to be very sure of what he was agreeing to.

"You see," explained Thomas, thinking quickly, "my friend, Helmud, has the most ferocious roar of any creature around and we'd like to let the queen hear it."

Mr. Smith nodded his head in great satisfaction. The sentry examined Helmud closely. He seemed to remain quite skeptical.

"Is that so?" he questioned.

"Yes," answered Thomas. "Would you like to hear it?"

The sentry nodded his head and Mr. Smith nodded his head, so Thomas turned to Helmud and nodded his head.

"Are you sure?" Helmud asked hesitantly.

"Yes," said Thomas.

"You won't run away?" worried Helmud.

"No," reassured his friend.

"Well?" interrupted the sentry very impatiently. "Will he growl or won't he?"

"It will be a roar, actually," answered Thomas politely.

"Well, I'm waiting," snapped the sentry. His ball was getting ever so much larger, as was Mr. Smith's.

Thomas again turned toward Helmud and nodded.

Helmud took a deep breath and roared one of his better roars. It was so ferocious that everyone nearby tried to run away. Everywhere, people in balls and chains were getting their balls and chains tangled up as they tried to escape. The sentry ducked behind his guardhouse and Mr. Smith even tried to join him.

After the commotion calmed down, the sentry crawled out from behind the guardhouse and opened the door to the throne room.

"Y-y-you may enter," he stammered.

Thomas nodded as he and Helmud marched past. Mr. Smith followed them, shaken somewhat by the roar, but looking triumphant. The sentry frowned back at him and Mr. Smith's ball grew just a tiny bit larger.

The trio walked down a short hallway and right into the throne room. Once inside, Thomas was amazed by how ornate the room was. It had high ceilings and a number of intricately woven tapestries hanging from the walls.

The throne room was abuzz with noise and activity. Members of the queen's entourage were continually coming and going. There were small pockets of people talking with each other and guards lined both sides of the large room, ensuring that everyone behaved in a fitting manner in the queen's presence.

Queen Juliana sat on a high throne. Even her feet were above Thomas' eye level. She was an older lady with sagging eyelids, and Thomas thought she looked a bit like Mrs. Green from school. Her hair was curled and she was dressed in a royal robe that looked just like what Thomas imagined a queen would wear.

On the queen's left sat her ball and chain. The ball was larger than any Thomas had seen previously. He was almost certain that Queen Juliana couldn't walk at all, or only if she had a lot of help.

Thomas began to wish that he and Helmud hadn't agreed to visit the City of Bitterness and he wondered how they might escape.

Queen Juliana

XII

Queen Juliana

Thomas and Helmud watched as crowd of attendants stood around the queen's throne, continually giving her sympathy and tissues.

"Oh," cried the queen, "The king treated me so badly!"

"Yes," replied an attendant. "He was very mean."

"He should have been put in the dungeon," said another.

"What he did was inexcusable," chimed in a third.

"Oh, my," said Thomas to no one in particular. Turning to Mr. Smith, he asked, "What did the king do?"

"Oh, it was awful," Mr. Smith replied. "Horrible."

"What was it?"

"The king forgot the queen's birthday! He didn't get her a present or even a card."

Thomas nodded gravely. He remembered once when his father had done that on his mother's birthday. Life at home was no fun for a few weeks after that.

"When did the king forget her birthday?" Thomas asked.

"It was 32 years, 5 months, 1 week and 3 days ago."

Thomas' eyes widened. "32 years?"

"And 5 months, 1 week and 3 days ago," repeated Mr. Smith flatly, but emphatically.

"Where is the king now?" Thomas asked.

"Oh, he has been dead for at least 15 years."

Their conversation was interrupted as the queen burst into great tears all over again. Attendants hustled and bustled about, attempting to soothe her. At that moment, Queen Juliana noticed Mr. Smith, Thomas and Helmud.

"And who are these visitors?" she declared in her most regal voice.

All of the queen's attendants looked at each other in fear and turned to stare at the trio of newcomers.

Mr. Smith nervously stepped forward and bowed, "My majestic and wonderful Queen," he began, "these two are Thomas and his companion, Helmud. I met them just outside the city."

"I remember when I could go outside the city," the queen mourned sadly, tears coming to her eyes. "It must be even more beautiful now than it was before."

The queen began sobbing. Her attendants rushed about with tissues and kind words to placate her.

"Oh, my Queen, it's not your fault," declared one.

"It will all be fine," soothed another.

The queen blew her nose and seethed angrily, "If that king had only treated me properly, my life would have been wonderful!"

She thumped her fist against the arm of her throne. As she did, her ball grew larger. Attendants quickly ran to the queen's side to offer even more sympathy.

Once the queen had finally calmed down, she ordered her visitors to come forward and introduce themselves. Thomas and Helmud hesitated for a moment and then cautiously walked up beside Mr. Smith.

"And who are you again?" Queen Juliana demanded.

"I'm Thomas," Thomas said, bowing awkwardly. "And this is my friend, Helmud the hudlunk."

"What brings you to the City of Bitterness?"

"Mr. Smith invited us to visit, your Majesty," Thomas answered. "We are traveling to the Land of Freedom."

"Freedom!" the queen cried out. "Oh, to be free again! But I will never be free, and it's all the king's fault!"

Queen Juliana began sobbing again. Thomas felt sorry for her. She seemed to be very lonely and miserable, even with all of her attendants.

Finally, the queen regained her composure. She then interrupted Thomas' thoughts, saying, "And why have you come to visit me? Are you here to offer condolences for what the king did to me?"

Mr. Smith quickly cleared his throat. "Your Majesty, I met these two on the road outside the city and . . ."

"Outside the city," the queen sighed, tears coming to her eyes. Immediately, the tearful scene from before began to repeat itself.

"I remember when I could go outside the city," Queen Juliana sobbed. "It must be even more beautiful now than it was before."

"As I was saying, your Majesty," Mr. Smith interrupted. "I met these two on the road outside the city and . . ."

The queen burst into tears all over again. "I wish I could go outside the city," she cried.

The queen's attendants rushed to her aid.

"It will all be fine," declared one.

"Oh, my queen, it's not your fault," soothed another. "It is all the king's fault."

"You are right," Queen Juliana seethed angrily. "If the king had treated me nicely, I would be happy now!"

This time, the queen stood up and declared, "He must pay for all he did!"

"The play! The play!" shouted one attendant. Soon, more joined in, filling the room with their urgent cries.

Actors and actresses rushed in and began performing a play, titled *All the Evils of the King*. As he watched, Thomas sensed that this play must have been presented to the queen many times before – perhaps daily.

The plot was confusing, but as best as he could tell, the entire play revolved around the birthday incident from 32 years, 5 months, 1 week and 3 days before.

At the end of the play, Queen Juliana thumped her fist on her throne. The ball and chain she wore grew larger and she bellowed, "That king must pay for his crimes!"

The throne room was immediately astir with various attendants rushing about trying to calm the queen down.

Thomas leaned over to Helmud. "How will we ever get out of here?" he moaned.

Helmud growled. He didn't know how to escape either.

Thomas began to get irritated at Mr. Smith. Turning to Helmud, he complained, "If Mr. Smith hadn't brought us in here, everything would be fine right now."

Helmud nodded, shaking his mane in frustration.

Then, as if by magic, a ball and chain suddenly appeared around the left ankles of both the boy and the hudlunk.

Helmud Roars

XIII

Escape from the City of Bitterness

Thomas and Helmud looked at each other and their balls and chains in shock.

"*This can't be happening!*" thought Thomas. He began to get more upset at Mr. Smith, and, as he did, his ball and chain grew even larger. Helmud tried to run away, but he could barely move.

For the first time, Mr. Smith acknowledged the presence of the balls and chains, instructing them, "Don't worry. It's hard to drag now, but you'll get used to it. You won't even notice that it is there."

Thomas angrily replied, "Well, I don't ever want to get used to it. This is all your fault!"

In an instant, his ball grew even larger.

Thomas stared in disbelief. He could hardly move! His dismay turned to anger as he looked at Mr. Smith.

"You knew this would happen!" Thomas said to Mr. Smith accusingly, his ball growing larger as he spoke.

Mr. Smith replied defiantly, "It's your own fault! Don't blame me!"

Mr. Smith's ball also grew larger.

Thomas tried to stomp away, but dragging the ball was very hard. He managed to move it only a yard or two at most. One of the queen's attendants noticed Thomas' predicament and said sincerely, "It's a terrible thing that Mr. Smith did to you."

Thomas grew even angrier at Mr. Smith. He began to think of even more mean things he could yell at the man. As he did, Thomas was shocked to see his ball get even bigger. He tried to move it, but now the ball was so large that Thomas couldn't go even a single step. The boy looked at it in utter dismay. Feeling hopeless, Thomas sat down with his back against the ball.

"I've lost my way to freedom," he groaned.

Several attendants quickly appeared. They each offered tissues and words of sympathy.

"It will all be fine," comforted one.

"Oh, young man, it's not your fault," soothed another.

"It's all Mr. Smith's fault. He's the one who has to fix this mess," offered a third.

Thomas angrily agreed and immediately felt the ball growing behind him.

He looked around for Mr. Smith, but he was nowhere to be seen. Finally, Thomas spotted him standing across the room with his back toward Thomas and his arms folded tightly. His ball had grown larger, too. Thomas tried to drag his ball to Mr. Smith, but it was impossible.

Discouraged, he looked for Helmud. The hudlunk was much closer, but his ball had grown quite large as well. Thomas tried to crawl over to his friend, but his chain was only long enough to reach halfway there. Calling to Helmud, Thomas was able to get the hudlunk to meet him at the very end of each of their chains.

"What are we going to do?" asked Thomas, who was on the verge of tears.

"If Mr. Smith comes back this way, I think I'll take a bite out of his leg," growled Helmud. "Then, maybe I'll roar as loud as I can and empty this entire room. They all deserve it."

As he watched Helmud getting angrier and angrier, Thomas realized that he was the one who had brought the hudlunk into the City of Bitterness. Helmud had trusted Thomas' leadership and Thomas had failed him.

Looking sadly at the hudlunk, the boy said, "Helmud, I brought you in here and that was a mistake. I'm sorry."

Helmud's eyes softened. "That's okay," he answered.

Instantly, the hudlunk's ball shrank. It shrank just a tiny bit, but it shrank nonetheless. Thomas and Helmud both looked at it in astonishment.

Then Thomas thought about the time when his little sister broke his favorite toy and his mother told him to forgive her. It was a hard thing to do, but he did feel better afterwards. Now, Thomas had an idea!

After waving to Mr. Smith for several minutes, Thomas was able to catch his attention. Still angry, Mr. Smith nevertheless marched over to the boy and glared at him. Thomas then stood up and mustered his courage.

"Mr. Smith," he announced, "I was angry with you for bringing us here, but I forgive you."

As he spoke those words, Thomas' ball started to shrink! Emboldened, he forgave Mr. Smith for everything he could think of. As he did, Thomas' ball got smaller and smaller. Helmud also began to forgive Mr. Smith and Thomas. Soon, both of their balls and chains had almost completely disappeared.

The throne room came to a standstill as everyone was drawn to the spectacle. No one had ever seen anything like this before! After just a few moments, though, the queen's attendants rushed over to Thomas and Helmud, rebuking them.

"You can't do that!" one declared.

"It's not right!" cried another.

"He has to want to be forgiven!" demanded a third.

The chorus continued, growing louder and louder and louder. Everyone in the throne room seemed very angry that Thomas and Helmud had forgiven Mr. Smith.

"You deserve to be angry."

"He needs to get what's coming to him!"

"Don't let him off easy! That's not fair!"

"You have every right to be hurt!"

"He needs to make it up to you!"

Thomas looked around in desperation. Neither he nor Helmud had a ball and chain anymore, but the crush of people around them made it impossible to move.

"Roar!" yelled Thomas to Helmud. "Roar!"

Helmud nodded his head and took a deep breath. Then he released one of the loudest, most ferocious, most menacing roars he had ever roared in all of his roaring days.

"RRROOOAAARRR!"

Helmud's roar was absolutely deafening! It reverberated throughout the throne room, terrifying everyone present. The queen's attendants all crouched on the floor beside their balls, trembling with fear. Quickly, Thomas called to Helmud and they began to run from the throne room.

Queen Juliana was the first to recover from the shock of the roar. Rising up, she screamed, "Stop! You two! I command you to stop!"

Thomas and Helmud ignored the queen. They sprinted out of the throne room and past the sentry as fast as they could. As they left, Thomas heard the queen cry out, "They have ruined my day! It's all their fault for making me feel so miserable!"

*"Welcome to Denial.
It's the most beautiful land around."*

XIV

The Wasteland of Denial

The pair ran through the city and out the front gates. Turning right, they raced down the road until both were exhausted. Seeing no pursuers, Thomas and Helmud finally stopped to rest by the side of the road. It was getting dark now, too, so the pair decided to spend the night in the woods beside the road before continuing on.

That next morning, they both awoke feeling renewed and re-energized. Before starting out, Thomas opened his backpack and took out the lantern. He wanted to make sure it was still in good condition.

"What is that?" Helmud asked.

"This is the Lantern of Elsdat. I'm supposed to carry it to the Land of Freedom. The wizard said that I can go home if I do," Thomas replied.

The hudlunk sniffed at it for a moment.

"It looks like a plain old lamp to me. I doubt that it even works very well. Why do you have to take something this useless to the Land of Freedom?"

"I don't know, but if I have to take it there to get home, then that's what I'm going to do," Thomas replied.

As he looked down the road, Thomas was surprised to see the beautiful countryside give way to a desolate land ahead. It didn't look appealing at all.

Thomas thought about his journey so far and reminded himself that it was better to face his difficulties than it was to go looking for shortcuts. Standing up, he put on his backpack and motioned to Helmud.

"Come on," he said. "Let's get this part of the journey over with. It's not going to go away."

Helmud groaned. "Do we really have to go this way?" he complained.

"Yes," said Thomas firmly. "We do."

As the pair walked along, they came to a billboard with a map depicting the desolate land ahead of them. As Thomas stopped to study it, he discovered that the land was really two separate places. Over the picture of the wasteland on the left side of the road was a label that proclaimed:

Wasteland of Denial

Underneath, in small letters, it read:

Ignorance is bliss. Denial is close.

On the right side of the road, there was a mud flat that was labeled:

Hopeless Hollow

"Neither one looks very nice," Thomas said to Helmud.

Before the hudlunk could answer, a man stepped out from behind the map and announced, "Why, that's not true. This is the most beautiful land around."

Helmud was so surprised that he nearly bit the man. The man simply smiled at the hudlunk. He extended his hand to Thomas and gave Helmud a scratch behind the ears. Nothing seemed to bother him in the least.

"Welcome to Denial," he continued. "As I said, it's the most beautiful land around."

The man motioned with his hand to the wasteland on the left. "Isn't it gorgeous?" he declared. "That's my house right over there."

Thomas looked to where the man was pointing. It took a moment for him to realize that the man was referring to an old, rundown shack just a short distance away.

"This way," the man said. "Come meet my wife."

"Okay," said Thomas as he and Helmud started to walk with the man. "I'm Thomas. What's your name?"

The man smiled at the boy happily, "My name is Henry, Happy Henry. But most folks just call me Henry."

"This is Helmud."

"I'm very pleased to meet you both," said Henry.

Soon, they reached the shack. Henry led them into the only room of the house. It was lit by a single light bulb hanging from the ceiling. In a corner was a smoky potbellied stove. A woman stood there, stirring something that gurgled in a big, black pot. It smelled awful.

"Hi, Honey!" the man proclaimed cheerfully as they entered the dilapidated house.

The woman scowled at him and kept stirring.

"I brought some new friends home for lunch," he said. "I knew you wouldn't mind."

Turning to his company, the man continued, "This is my wife, Tina."

"Honey," he said to her, "this is Thomas and his friend, Helmud."

Tina glanced up from the cooking pot and nodded her head curtly, but she didn't say a word.

While lunch was being fixed, Henry and his guests sat down. Thomas and Henry took the only two chairs, wooden ones, and Helmud chose a box.

"See?" said Henry. "I told you this is a great house!"

Trying to be a courteous guest, Thomas asked, "How long have you lived here?"

"Not long enough," Henry laughed. "It has been about twenty years – ever since the children left."

Tina spoke up for the only time, "You mean when they died in the accident."

"Maybe it was twenty-one years," Henry continued as if Tina had never spoken. "It's hard to keep track of time in a place as wonderful as this."

A moment later, Tina served lunch. Thomas, who had been taught that he had to try everything on his plate, looked down in dismay at the stew she had served. It was a watery gray broth with little brown chunks of something floating in it. It smelled like the locker room at school. Helmud, too, frowned at his food.

"I can tell you're going to love this!" declared Henry. "Just the look on your faces as you smell Tina's great stew tells me you're going to think this is delicious."

Over the next few minutes, Henry entertained his guests with stories about how wonderful it was living in the wasteland. Thomas thought to himself that it was almost impossible to believe that Henry was talking about the same place as the one they were in right then.

Finally, to be polite, Thomas attempted a sip of his stew. It was worse than he had imagined. He actually gagged while trying to swallow it.

Henry nodded knowingly. "That's what happens to most people who eat here. The food is just a bit too rich for them, I imagine."

Thomas and Helmud exchanged glances. Then, as Henry kept talking, Helmud hid his bowl behind his box. A swarm of flies immediately descended on it.

Thomas covered his bowl with a dingy napkin. Even the smell of the food was making his stomach queasy. The boy tried to look attentively at Henry.

After listening to Henry talk for an hour longer, Thomas decided that it was time to go. He attempted to excuse himself and Helmud.

"We must be going," he said. "We don't want to impose on your hospitality and we have quite a journey still ahead of us."

"Really?" Henry commented as they got up and left the house. "Where are you going?"

"To the Land of Freedom."

Henry laughed, "You can go there if you want, but why would you?"

Then, waving his arms over the wasteland, he continued, "As you can see, we have everything a person could want right here."

Henry then bent down and looked Thomas in the eye. "You don't really want to go further," he said intently. "It's dangerous and you may fail. It's better to stay right here than it is to go on."

"Besides," he continued, "living here is where you will have true freedom. Freedom isn't found in being able to do more. There is always more to do and it keeps you trapped. Freedom is found in being content with what you have."

Thomas looked doubtfully at Henry. Something about him made the boy's spine shiver.

Thomas was sure that the Wasteland of Denial wasn't for him. He would never be able to live in a pretend freedom. Besides, he felt certain that there was more to freedom than just giving up and settling for a tumbledown shack and gray stew. There had to be a better freedom than that.

Resolutely, the boy shook Henry's hand and told him goodbye. He and Helmud returned to the road and continued onward.

After they had traveled some distance away, the two companions began to talk to each other.

"That food was terrible," Helmud complained.

"It was the worst food I've ever eaten," agreed Thomas.

"And this is really a miserable place, not a beautiful one," Helmud continued.

"Yes," Thomas replied.

Helmud kicked a rock along the path.

"I wonder why Henry thinks it's so great."

"I don't know," Thomas answered. "Maybe sometimes it's easier to just pretend, especially when there's a problem you don't think you can change. I did that once when we moved to a new city."

Helmud nodded in understanding and then sighed. Thomas guessed that the hudlunk was thinking about his family.

It was too late

XV

Muddling Through

Thomas and Helmud continued along the road toward the Land of Freedom. As they walked, Thomas gazed at Hopeless Hollow. The mud flat extended as far as he could see. Way off in the distance, Thomas was able to make out some low hills that he hoped marked the end of this miserable land.

The mud flat itself seemed to be a broad, flat plain made of slimy mud. There were no plants and no outcroppings of any kind. Thomas wondered how far he could slide in the mud if he got a running start.

"Hey," Thomas said, "wouldn't that be fun to slide on?"

Helmud shook his mane. "No, thanks. You can try, but I wouldn't want to fall into one of those holes."

"Holes?" Thomas was surprised.

Helmud pointed with his paw and Thomas saw for the first time that there were holes dotting the mud flat.

Thomas stopped to stare out at them.

Most of the holes were far from the road, so there was little he could actually tell about them. Some were quite small in diameter, while others seemed as wide as a crater on the moon. It was hard to tell how deep they were without getting a closer look.

"Let's keep going," sighed Thomas, less confidently than before. The mud flat seemed to stretch on forever and he was feeling a bit dismayed at how far they had to go. Thomas even began wondering if they would ever make it to the Land of Freedom.

After walking for many hours, it seemed to Thomas and Helmud that they hadn't gotten any closer to the end of the mud flat. To make things worse, the taste of their last meal, the gray stew, was still stuck in their mouths. It seemed as if it would never leave. Helmud was getting more and more discouraged.

"Do we really need to go this way? Couldn't we just go back?" he begged. "It would be a whole lot easier."

"No," answered Thomas hesitantly as he adjusted his backpack. "This is the only way to get to the Land of Freedom. I don't think we should turn back."

Helmud looked forlornly over his shoulder. He really wanted to go home. The hudlunk even contemplated leaving Thomas and going back by himself.

The problem was that he was too scared to go back alone. Helmud felt trapped. He didn't want to keep going and he couldn't make Thomas go back. Helmud's gloomy thoughts went round and round until Thomas' voice finally interrupted them.

"Look! It's one of the holes!" said Thomas.

Sure enough, up ahead there was a mud pit. It looked to be about medium-sized, so it was nothing special – except that it was close to the road. The two of them would be able to look down inside it.

After a few minutes of walking briskly, they arrived at the pit. It looked to be about fifty feet across. Thomas was astounded to see that it wasn't shallow at all. The mud pit was at least thirty feet deep!

As they peered over the edge, Thomas and Helmud were even more surprised to find a man sitting at the bottom. He was coated in dried mud and was staring dismally at the ground.

"Do you need any help?" Thomas called down. The boy had no idea how he and Helmud could help the man, but Thomas was sure he could think of something.

Thomas thought that the man would welcome the chance to be rescued, but he didn't move an inch. Instead, the man continued to sit still and lamented, "It's hopeless. There is no way out of these pits. Just keep going. Don't even bother to try and help me."

"What do you mean, it's hopeless?"

"As I said," the man replied sadly. "There is no way out. I've tried every way to escape and nothing works."

"Has anyone ever offered to help you before?" offered Thomas optimistically.

"No, but I know it won't work," the man assured him with growing irritation in his voice.

Thomas stepped gingerly off the road to get closer to the edge of the pit. He and Helmud had not previously ventured onto the mud, so he was a bit worried about what it would be like. To the boy's surprise, the ground became firm under his feet.

"Come on!" he cried to the man. "If we can find a rope or something, I think we can pull you out."

The man hardly looked up. "No, thank you," he sighed dejectedly. "It's no use."

Helmud walked over to Thomas. His paws were sinking slightly in the mud.

"He's right," the hudlunk agreed. "There is no way to get him out of there."

Thomas gasped in horror as Helmud began sinking even further into the mud. In seconds, a mud pit formed around the hudlunk as he sank deeper and deeper.

"Get back on the road!" Thomas commanded.

It was too late. Helmud was now in a pit that was nearly fifteen feet deep, and the mud at the bottom had risen up to his knees. Not only that, but the pit was growing with each passing second.

"There's no way out," Helmud growled miserably. "I'm trapped in here forever."

Thomas felt helpless as he watched his friend sink even more. There seemed to be nothing he could do to help! As the boy grew more discouraged, the ground beneath him started turning to mud. He was sinking, too!

Thomas tried to scramble back to the path, but he was already several feet deep in mud. In desperation, he tried everything he could think of to get himself out of the pit.

Unfortunately, the more frantic and worried Thomas became, the more he sank down in the mud. Finally, he stopped fighting. He was already in a mud pit that was at least 20 feet deep.

"How in the world will I ever get out of here?" Thomas said sadly to himself.

Thomas in the Mud

XVI

In the Pits

Thomas sat in his mud pit, feeling very discouraged as he listened to Helmud groaning nearby.

"Well, isn't this just great!" the man griped from the bottom of his pit. "As if this mud pit isn't bad enough, now I no longer have any peace and quiet."

Thomas sighed and began to assess the situation more fully. He and Helmud were trapped in separate mud pits. The sides were so smooth and slippery that it seemed impossible to climb out.

Thomas' discouragement deepened. As it did, he felt himself sinking into the mud a little bit more. The boy was knee deep in mud and felt almost completely hopeless about ever escaping. He could tell by listening to his friend's howls that Helmud felt the same way. After struggling to free himself for almost an hour, Thomas finally quit fighting.

He sat down in the mud, completely motionless. Then, as Thomas looked around at the mud walls, somehow his feelings started to change. He was no longer filled with despair. Instead, he was mad. Thomas resolved to find a way of escape. Speaking out loud, he declared, "I'm going to get out of here!"

The moment he spoke, Thomas felt the mud around him become a bit more solid than it was before. When that happened, his excitement grew. As he became more hopeful, Thomas felt the mud getting even more solid. Quickly, the boy pulled himself up out of the mud. He was soon sitting on solid ground at the bottom of the mud pit.

Thomas thought about what had just happened. It occurred to him that when he had hope, the ground stayed solid, but if he began to lose hope, the ground turned into mud. Suddenly, Thomas realized that hope was the key to escaping from the mud pit!

"Why," he declared excitedly, "I'm going to make a set of stairs and walk right out of here!"

Thomas placed his right foot against the wall of the pit. As he did, the ground under his foot turned solid and he was able to take a step up. Emboldened, Thomas took another step. The same thing happened!

Now he was certain he could get out. All Thomas had to do was place one foot after the other, one step at a time. In fact, in just a matter of seconds he had reached the top of the pit and climbed completely out. In his excitement, he immediately thought of running over to tell Helmud.

But something stopped him. How was Thomas going to get Helmud out? He thought of climbing in the pit with Helmud and having the hudlunk walk out after him, but

Thomas was afraid that Helmud wouldn't be able to get out that way. Maybe in order to escape, the hudlunk would have to have his own hope.

"*That's it!*" Thomas told himself. "*What Helmud needs is hope!*"

Thomas lay down on the ground right near the edge of Helmud's mud pit. He stayed back just enough so that he couldn't be seen.

"Hey! Helmud!" he called out.

"Grrrmumph," came back the depressing reply.

Helmud's growl was so depressing that Thomas felt himself starting to sink in the mud.

"Be quiet," Thomas commanded. "And listen to me."

"Grrrmumph . . . grrr."

This time, Thomas laughed at Helmud's answer and he didn't sink a bit.

"Helmud! I'm in a mud pit just like you, right?"

"Yeah."

"What if I told you I found a way to get out? Would you believe me?"

"No," came the flat reply.

"Not at all?"

"No. There is no way out of these pits. We are trapped in here forever."

"Come on!" Thomas urged his friend. "There must be something I can do to make you believe that we can get out of this mud!"

"I won't believe it unless I see you standing at the top of my pit, waving your arms at me and dancing," came the depressed reply.

That was just what Thomas had been waiting for. The boy jumped to his feet, stood at the edge of Helmud's pit, and stared down at the hudlunk.

"Here I am!" Thomas cried out, waving his arms and dancing around. "See, you can get out!"

Helmud's eyes widened, and for a split second, they lit up with hope. Seeing that, Thomas ordered him, "Get up and start climbing. Don't think! Just do it! Now! You can climb right out of that pit!"

Shocked by Thomas' forcefulness, Helmud took a step up the side of the pit. As he did, the ground grew firm beneath his paws and his eyes widened in surprise.

"See!" Thomas exclaimed excitedly. "You can get out of that pit!"

Encouraged, Helmud took another step, then another, and another. Soon, he, too, was out of the pit and back on solid ground. The boy and the hudlunk grabbed each other in celebration.

"We did it!" exclaimed Helmud.

"We sure did!" Thomas laughed. "Let's get out of this place before something else happens!"

"What about him?" the hudlunk asked, looking back at the other mud pit in sympathy.

"Do you want to get out of your pit?" Thomas called out to the man. "We just escaped! You can, too! It's easy!"

"Don't play games with me!" the man yelled irritably. "I know you were never in a pit in the first place. You are just trying to torment me by making me hope again. Well, I've had enough of hope. It's useless. Having hope just leads to more disappointment."

After Thomas had pleaded for several more minutes, the man got very angry and shouted at him to shut up and leave. He even began throwing globs of mud at Thomas and Helmud. Saddened, the boy and his hudlunk friend turned away. They got back on the road to continue their journey to the Land of Freedom.

"That food is cold."

XVII

The Maze of Approval

The remainder of their passage through the wasteland went much more quickly. Thomas and Helmud enjoyed each other's company and did their best to stay on the road. Thomas occasionally shifted the backpack he was wearing to make it more comfortable.

"Do you want me to carry it for you?" Helmud asked.

"No, thank you," Thomas replied. "I think that I should carry the backpack. That's what the wizard said to do."

As the sun began to go down, the pair finally found themselves at the edge of the wasteland. They crossed over a small hill and came upon what appeared to be some kind of orchard. It was getting dark and there was no house or caretaker nearby, only rows of trees laden with ripe fruit.

"Do you know what these are?" asked Thomas.

"No," replied Helmud, who was eagerly eating some of the fruit. "But they taste delicious."

Thomas paused for just a moment and then pulled some fruit off a tree for himself. After eating their fill, the pair settled down to sleep for the night.

The next morning, Thomas was awakened by an old man prodding him on the shoulder with a cane.

"What are you doing here?" the old man demanded. "Have you been eating my fruit?"

Thomas shook himself awake and tried to apologize, but the old man would have nothing of it.

"You have stolen fruit from my orchard," he stated emphatically, "and now you must pay for it!"

Thomas explained that he would gladly pay for the food, but he had no money.

"Then you will have to work to pay your debt off," the man said sternly. "Consider yourself lucky that I'm not calling the constable to take you away. Follow me."

Sheepishly, Helmud and Thomas followed the man. After they had walked for about fifteen minutes, the road took a sharp turn through a grove of trees. There, before them, lay a driveway leading up to a large mansion. On the front lawn was what appeared to be a maze made of high, trimmed hedges. It looked like one of the mazes that Thomas had seen in books at school.

Over the driveway was an archway. It was made out of large stones and had a sign suspended from the top of the arch. In bright blue lettering it read:

House of Rooval, Reginald Rooval, Owner

Thomas thought to himself, *"This old man must be Reginald Rooval."*

He couldn't help but snicker, wondering if this particular old man ever played knick-knack paddy-whack.

"What are you laughing at?" the old man demanded. "Stop it now and get to work!"

Thomas looked down penitently.

"Yes sir. What work would you like us to do?"

Mr. Rooval eyed him sternly.

"Your job," he said, "is to go to the kitchen, get my wife's breakfast from the cook, and bring it to her in the maze. You must be quick about it or the food will get cold. Do a good job or I'll make you stay and fix any messes you make."

Neither Helmud nor Thomas wanted to stay any longer than they had to, so they hurried off to the kitchen.

It turned out that hurrying to the kitchen and finding the kitchen were two completely different things. The pair searched nearly every room on the first floor before they found an angry old butler who told them that the kitchen was in the attic. Scurrying up the stairs, they arrived just in time to be yelled at by the cook because Mrs. Rooval's breakfast had gotten cold.

"What took you so long?" she demanded. "Now I have to fix Mrs. Rooval's breakfast all over again."

Discouraged, Thomas sat down to wait. As he did, the old man came up the stairs.

"What are you doing sitting around?" he scolded. "You need to get that breakfast to my wife right away!"

Thomas tried to explain, but Mr. Rooval would have none of it. He glared at the boy and walked away.

"Here you are," snapped the cook as she handed Thomas a new tray of food. "Now, hurry up!"

Thomas and Helmud began to run down the stairs with the breakfast tray for Mrs. Rooval. They had only gone down one flight, though, when the butler saw them.

"No running in the house!" he ordered.

Obediently, Thomas and Helmud started walking down the stairs. There were several flights to go and Thomas was afraid that the food would get cold. As it was, he was spotted by the old man just a few steps later.

"What are you doing walking?" he shouted. "You need to deliver that food to my wife as fast as possible!"

In an effort to please Mr. Rooval, Helmud offered to carry Thomas on his back. In this way, they bounded down the stairs very quickly, only to be stopped at the bottom by another maid.

"What are you doing playing?" she demanded. "There is no running or playing in the mansion. Now carry that food out to Mrs. Rooval right away."

Not ten steps later, Mr. Rooval appeared with a look of stern disapproval. He sniffed at the breakfast tray.

"That food is cold," he said angrily. "Go back upstairs and get some more."

Greatly discouraged, Thomas and Helmud turned around and started up the staircase. When they finally reached the kitchen, the cook scolded them again and announced that there were no more eggs so she couldn't fix another breakfast. They would have to take the food they had to Mrs. Rooval and that was that.

Thomas and Helmud turned to go downstairs again. Just as they arrived at the first floor, the pair was accosted by the butler who examined the food for himself.

"This simply will not do," he said, glaring at them. "You must go back and try again."

Wearily, Thomas and Helmud turned around to go back upstairs once more. By now, they had gone up and down the stairs twice each way. They had run; they had walked; and Thomas had even gotten a ride on Helmud, but nothing satisfied these people! Thomas gritted his teeth. He knew he could do the job well if he tried just a bit harder.

When they reached the kitchen, Thomas and Helmud were met by Mr. Rooval, who reprimanded them, "It's your fault that my wife missed breakfast. Here is a cold glass of tea with five ice cubes just the way she likes it. You had better deliver this to her before the ice melts."

"Let's take the middle entrance."

XVIII

Iced Tea

Thomas took the glass of iced tea and hurried downstairs with Helmud. This time, they walked very fast, not quite fast enough to be running but also not quite slow enough to be walking. In this way, they managed to pass under the watchful eyes of the butler and two maids. Once out on the front yard, the two companions looked at each other in confusion.

"Where do we go now?" asked Helmud.

"I don't know," answered Thomas. "Mrs. Rooval is in the maze, but I don't know how to get to her."

Thomas and Helmud studied their options. There were three entrances to the maze, but none of them looked any better than the other two.

"Let's take the middle entrance," Helmud suggested.

Thomas agreed and they entered the maze. After just a short distance, they found an intersection and turned right. A few yards later, however, there was a sign hanging between the hedges. It read:

No Entrance

Obediently, they turned around to go the other way. The path wound around and doubled back so often that Thomas was soon completely disoriented. He had no idea where they needed to go to reach Mrs. Rooval, nor could he tell where the maze had even started.

"What do you think?" he asked Helmud.

"Let's go this way," the hudlunk suggested.

After five more minutes of fruitless wandering, Thomas couldn't tell if they had made any progress at all.

"Let's try this way now," Helmud offered, pointing back to the way from which they had just come.

Thomas was sure that it would do them no good, but he agreed anyway. To his shock, as they retraced their steps Thomas discovered that the path through the maze was now different than it was just a few minutes before!

Stopping, he said to Helmud, "Wait a minute."

The pair tip-toed to the next turn in the maze. After several moments, Thomas heard a rustling in the bushes around the corner. He and Helmud jumped out just in time to see the hedges changing their positions!

"Look, Helmud!" Thomas said, pointing to the ground. The bushes had no roots and could move around at will. They had been playing tricks on the pair the entire time.

Thomas stared at the bushes in astonishment. He had never seen walking hedges before. Talking trees had been bad enough, but this was ridiculous!

Indignantly, Thomas faced the row of bushes in front of him and ordered, "We need to get this tea to Mrs. Rooval right away! Either you clear a path for us or we will tear your branches off you until you do!"

There was a moment of utter quiet. Then, Thomas began to reach for the nearest bush. As he did, the other bushes started to move away. They created a walkway from Thomas and Helmud to Mrs. Rooval. She was now in plain view, not more than fifteen feet away.

Mrs. Rooval was a slightly heavy lady. She was sitting in a lounge chair and there was a small table beside her, upon which sat a book and a coaster. Thomas assumed, correctly, that he should place her drink there.

The pair walked up, nodded a greeting, set the iced tea down, and turned to go. They hadn't gone more than a few feet when Mrs. Rooval called for them to come back.

"Where's my sugar?" she demanded.

"Sugar?" asked Thomas.

"Yes, sugar. I always have sugar with my tea."

"But they said the tea was exactly the way you wanted it," Thomas protested.

"Not today!" Mrs. Rooval replied defensively. "Today, I want sugar, just like I always do on days like today. You should have known that!"

Thomas let out a deep sigh. "*Boy!*" he thought. "*Trying to keep these people happy is impossible.*"

"What are you sighing for?" Mrs. Rooval asked sharply.

"Nothing, ma'am," Thomas replied politely.

"Have you gotten my sugar yet?"

"No, ma'am."

"Get me some coffee instead," ordered Mrs. Rooval.

Thomas turned to go, only to bump into Mr. Rooval who was walking into the center of the maze.

"You are a poor worker!" Mr. Rooval scolded Thomas. "You haven't gotten my wife breakfast or coffee. All you did was bring her some tea that she didn't want. What good are you?"

Thomas was completely dumbfounded. After all, it was Mr. Rooval who had told him to bring the tea in the first place. Thomas stood silently. Somehow, he didn't think that mentioning that fact would help the situation.

Then, behind him, Thomas heard a deep, low growl. He turned to see Helmud, with fire in his eyes, ready to pounce. The hudlunk opened his mouth and roared. It was just a medium roar, but it was enough to scare the Roovals.

Mrs. Rooval bolted out of her lawn chair in terror and screamed at the top of her lungs. It was a scream that seemed to echo for miles around. It was, in fact, an even more terrifying sound than Helmud's roar.

Mr. Rooval ran to his wife's side to assist her. She immediately grabbed a hold of his arm and begged for him to protect her.

"Save me from that animal!" she pleaded dramatically.

Mrs. Rooval fainted in her husband's arms. Thomas stepped forward to offer his assistance, but was brushed aside by Helmud.

"I'm hungry enough to eat both of you," he growled fiercely. Then Helmud leaped toward them and let out another roar. This time, it was one of his most ferocious.

Mr. Rooval, who had collapsed under the weight of his wife, trembled and pleaded for mercy. The bushes all backed away, leaving the couple all alone on the ground in front of Helmud and Thomas. Helmud stared fiercely down at Mr. Rooval.

"I think," Helmud said very deliberately, "that we have paid for the fruit we ate."

"Yes, yes," agreed Mr. Rooval, nodding his head vigorously.

Helmud continued, "I also think that you owe my friend an apology for how you have treated him."

Mr. Rooval whimpered out an apology. As apologies went, it wasn't a very good one, but Thomas accepted it nonetheless. He figured it may have been the first time Mr. Rooval had ever apologized.

Turning toward the bushes, Helmud roared and they scattered out of his way. Then, nodding to Thomas, the two of them walked slowly and calmly across the lawn, down the driveway, and away from the mansion.

Bridge at the Stream of Apathy

XIX

Wonderful Rest

Turning left at the end of the driveway, the two travelers continued on their journey. Thomas was glad to be away from the Rooval mansion and Helmud was delighted to not be sitting in a mud pit. The sun was high in the sky and a gentle breeze was blowing.

Soon, they approached a small stone bridge that crossed a stream. The bridge was engraved with the words:

Stream of Apathy

The stream itself gurgled invitingly. Helmud bounded across, but Thomas hesitated at the bridge for a moment.

"Come on," said Helmud. "The grass over here looks like a great place to stop and rest."

Thomas examined the bridge. It seemed solid enough so he ran quickly over it. Then, breathing a sigh of relief, he said, "I think you're right. Let's rest here a while."

There were fruit trees beside the stream and lush grass that grew along both banks. The grass appeared to be rather uneven, with lumpy mounds every now and then, but Thomas agreed that it looked like a perfect spot to take a break.

The hudlunk jumped down to the water for a cool drink. He was soon joined by Thomas and they both splashed about in the stream for several minutes. Then they wandered over to one of the fruit trees.

"Do you think Mr. Rooval owns these trees?" Thomas asked with a worried look on his face.

Helmud shook his head. "No, this kind grows wild. Let's have some for lunch!"

Thomas agreed and soon both of them were cheerfully munching away. Thomas had never eaten anything like this fruit before. It was shaped like an apple but tasted like the best melon he had ever eaten.

"Do you know what these are called, Helmud? I like them, whatever they are," Thomas commented happily.

"They're quislets," Helmud informed him, wiping his mouth with the back of his paw.

When they were done eating, Thomas lay down on his back while Helmud sprawled out on his stomach. The pair relaxed quietly beside the gurgling stream. It was very peaceful.

"I have a question," Helmud finally broke the silence.

"What is it?"

"I've been wondering why you keep that lantern in your backpack. It doesn't give much light that way."

"You're right," Thomas answered, taking the lantern out to inspect it. "When the wizard gave it to me, it was in the backpack. So I've just kept it there."

How does it stay lit? Does it use any fuel?"

"Not that I can tell," answered Thomas. "Sometimes it burns brightly and sometimes it is dim, but I haven't had to add any fuel to it."

"Does it ever get hot?"

Thomas lifted the glass around the light. It was certainly unusual, not like a flame, but not like a light bulb, either.

"Ouch!" he said. "It's hot when I remove the glass, but it's cool when the glass is in place."

Helmud sniffed the lantern and examined it closely.

"It still doesn't seem very special to me," the hudlunk finally commented.

"Me, neither. But if I'm ever going to get home, I have to get this lantern to the Land of Freedom." Thomas paused, "Oh, the lantern has a name, too."

"Really?"

"Yes. It's called the Lantern of Elsdat."

The name of the lantern meant nothing to Helmud. He rolled over and let out a low, peaceful purr.

By now, it was late afternoon. Thomas knew that a lot of time had passed, but he wanted to stay longer. Soon, the sun was setting and the two companions were still in the same place they had been since their arrival.

Helmud was ready to get moving, but Thomas seemed perfectly content. While he waited for Thomas to decide to leave, the hudlunk did a little exploring. First, he played in the stream again. Then he sniffed around at the fruit trees. Finally, the lumpy mounds in the grass attracted his attention.

The mounds were somewhat long, but not too high to jump over. They were placed haphazardly about, some close to each other and others far apart. The closest one to Helmud and Thomas was a number of yards away.

"Do you want to look at it with me?" Helmud asked.

"No," replied Thomas, yawning. "I think I'm going to take a little nap right here."

Helmud began sniffing his way to the nearest mound. He expected to find a pile of dirt covered in grass. As he approached it, however, the hudlunk suddenly stopped short. His eyes grew very focused and every part of his body went on full alert. The lump was alive!

After a moment, Helmud determined that the lump probably wasn't dangerous. Still, he remained cautious and approached it carefully, just in case. Then, Helmud discovered that the lump was actually a person who was completely covered with grass! The person was alive, but was either unable or unwilling to respond when Helmud spoke to it.

Bounding over to several of the other mounds, Helmud found that each one was another person covered entirely in grass. He tried talking to them, nudging them, even nibbling at their toes, but nothing caused the people to react in any way. Each one lay there, motionless. Their eyelids were closed and they were smiling in oblivion under their blanket of grass.

Helmud decided that he had seen enough. It was time to tell Thomas. Hurrying back, though, the hudlunk was horrified to see that the grass around Thomas was beginning to grow up over him. In fact, the boy was already partially covered!

"Thomas! Get up! We're in trouble!"

Thomas didn't move.

"No, we aren't," the boy finally replied in a very slow, groggy voice. "Everything is just fine."

"Thomas, the grass is trying to cover you up! You will become like these other lumps and never get to the Land of Freedom."

There was a long silence before Thomas responded.

"Who wants to go to the Land of Freedom anyway? This is such a nice place right here."

Helmud was sure that the grass was now covering even more of Thomas than it was just a few minutes ago.

"Your family! Thomas! You have to get back to your family!"

Again, there was a long silence. Finally, Thomas sighed, "Oh, my family is fine. I'm sure they will be alright without me."

Sniffing at a Mound of Grass

XX

Escape

Helmud didn't know what to do. With each passing minute Thomas was becoming less able to talk and even less interested in trying. Soon, he would look like all of the other lumps along the stream bank.

Helmud tried roaring. He howled. He pawed at Thomas. He even tried to drag Thomas away, but the boy was already completely covered with grass. There seemed to be no way for the hudlunk to free his friend. To make matters worse, the sun had now set and it was getting dark. Who knew what would happen then?

In desperation, Helmud picked up Thomas' backpack. Maybe there was something in there that could help. If nothing else, the lantern might provide some light.

"The lantern!" said Helmud to himself. *"That's it!"*

The hudlunk tore open the backpack and pulled out the lantern with his teeth. Helmud held the light up to look at Thomas. He was shocked to see that the boy was no longer even visible under the grass.

Frantically, Helmud tried to dig up the grass around Thomas, but it was no use. As hard as he pulled, the grass wouldn't budge. In fact, it felt to him as if the grass was pulling back.

Finally, Helmud made a desperate decision. Grabbing the lantern in his paws, he lifted off the glass shield and exposed the light. Maybe it would be hot enough to set the grass on fire!

Helmud tipped the lantern sideways and held the light to the grass. Immediately, the grass pulled away from it, but not for long. If he lifted the light up even a bit, the grass would move back in place. It didn't like the heat of the lantern, but it didn't catch fire, either. This was going to be a difficult battle!

Helmud hurried to a nearby quislet tree. With his strong teeth, he gnawed off a number of its slim branches. He took them back and began to lay them out in a large ring. Then the hudlunk held the light to the branches.

Helmud howled joyfully as he saw the branches began smoldering and then, one by one, they caught fire! As the branches burned, the long strands of grass pulled away from Thomas and disappeared underground. Soon, the boy was left lying in the dirt surrounded by a circle of burning branches.

Thomas sat up. He was very disoriented.

"Why is it so hot?" he mumbled, rubbing his eyes. The next moment, he saw the burning embers.

Jumping up in alarm, he called to Helmud, "We need to get out of here!"

Helmud jumped into the circle with Thomas.

"More than you know!" Helmud agreed. He began to explain to Thomas about the grass and the mounds along the stream bank. As everything Helmud told to him began to sink in, Thomas understood that the real danger wasn't the fire at all.

"How can we escape without walking on the grass?" Thomas worried.

"The grass doesn't seem to bother me. Why don't you climb on my back and I'll carry you?" Helmud offered. "If you hold the lantern so we can see, I can get you out of here to somewhere safe."

"That's a great idea!" exclaimed Thomas.

The boy got on the hudlunk's back and they leaped over the smoldering branches onto the grass. Thomas reached down to retrieve his backpack and the lantern. He replaced the glass and held the lantern out to light their way. All the while, he made sure not to touch the grass.

"It's a good thing you're a hudlunk!" Thomas said thankfully.

Helmud agreed and the two left the stream bank behind as quickly as possible. They journeyed by lantern light for over half an hour until they reached a rocky place with no grass growing on it. To Thomas, that seemed to be the only safe spot to spend the night. Tired from the day's adventures, the pair curled up on the rocks together and fell fast asleep.

Macroeconomics

XXI

A Busy Place

The next morning, Thomas was surprised to find that he and Helmud had spent the night not far from a large city. In fact, they were awakened early by the sound of a loud whistle. The pair sat up, rubbed their eyes and looked down at the city in the valley below.

Even from a distance, the place looked very busy. There were many large buildings, conveyor belts and twirling thing-a-ma-jigs as far as the eye could see.

It all seemed very exciting to Thomas and he was eager to get a better look. By now, he felt safe walking on his own, so the pair went side-by-side down the path.

Soon, they could read the big sign posted at the entrance to the city. It read:

Welcome to Macroeconomics

Idle Hands Are the Devil's Workshop

As they came to the city entrance, Thomas and Helmud could see right down the main street of town. Thomas paused in amazement. People were rushing back and forth, and forth and back, so quickly that it made his head spin.

"Wow!" he said to Helmud. "What a busy place! They must be doing something really important."

Helmud just stared in bewilderment.

As they were marveling at all of the activity, a very harried and important looking man rushed up to them.

"What are you doing wasting time?" he demanded. "There is too much to be done to just stand there doing nothing!"

"All we have is time, you know," he continued. "We must use our time wisely. And we are losing time every second. Hurry! Hurry! We need you over in Sector C."

Before they knew it, the man was pushing the pair down the city's main street. As they hurried, Thomas noticed that each block was identified by a letter of the alphabet; every building was labeled with a number; and each door had its own alphanumeric designator.

As a result, by the time they got to their destination, Thomas already knew that they were in Sector C, at Building 8, and in front of Door 54A. There was a sign on the door, proclaiming that it was a shoe factory.

"Hurry!" the man pleaded with them. "There isn't a moment to lose!"

Scurrying into the building, Thomas was amazed to find the largest factory he had ever seen. There were many people and a large number of conveyor belts carrying shoes and boxes back and forth across the warehouse.

At one end, people were opening the boxes and placing one left shoe in each box. Then, they would put the box onto a conveyor belt and it would zoom to the middle of the huge room. There, another group of people would open each box and add a right shoe. They would place the boxes in an elevator that took them to the top floor of the building.

At the top of the building, Thomas spotted a group of people hastily opening each box and dumping the shoes out onto another conveyor belt. Sorters on the conveyor line pulled out all of the right-footed shoes and threw them down a chute that deposited them right back in the middle of the room where they had started.

The rest of the shoes, the left-footed ones, traveled to the end of the conveyor where they were dropped down a different chute. This chute carried the shoes back to the left end of the room and placed them back in the pile they had originally come from.

As he looked more closely, Thomas saw yet another group of workers collecting shoes from the discard pile and taking them to a little room on the second floor. The door outside the room was Door 67A and had a sign which read:

Unlacing Room

Not more than four doors down, Thomas saw Door 68F with a sign that read:

Lacing Room

The boy looked on in confusion as shoes were taken from the pile on the warehouse floor and hauled to the unlacing room. Then, wheelbarrows of unlaced shoes were brought out and dumped on the conveyor belt, only to be sorted out a little bit later and sent to the lacing room. Meanwhile, shoelace couriers went from one room to the next with baskets of laces.

Somewhere in the middle of this bustle and activity, Thomas noticed yet another group. These people were very busy loading boxes of shoes onto a long conveyor belt that went out of the building.

"Where are those shoes going?" Thomas inquired.

"Off to the labeling plant," was the man's reply. "There, the boxes will be labeled and de-labeled and then re-labeled before they are sent to the taping building. Once taped, they will be sent to the de-taping facility. There all of the boxes in the city are opened and the contents are removed for shipment by either truck or conveyor belt back to their respective factories."

Sure enough, as Thomas watched, a truck arrived. It was filled with shoes, boxes and laces. As soon as the truck came to the door, a group of workers stopped what they were doing and rushed over to unload the truck.

"Aha!" said the man. "There is our problem! When the workers stop to unload the truck, it slows them down."

"Even worse," he continued urgently, "it slows everyone else down and almost brings the entire city to a complete standstill. We can't have that! If that ever happened, everything would fall apart!"

Turning to Thomas and Helmud, the man continued earnestly, "That's the place where we need you! We need someone to unload those trucks quickly. Get down there immediately and start unloading! It's the only way to save the city!"

Thomas and Helmud rushed to their positions. They emptied the first truck only to find that a second truck was just arriving. Working even harder, they managed to empty this second truck just before a third one pulled up with another full load.

The pair was moving as fast as they could, taking out shoes and tossing them onto Conveyor A2, placing laces in Bucket C431 and tossing the boxes down an ominous chute labeled:

Destruction Room, 132B

Just as they finished unloading the fourth truck, two more trucks arrived at the exact same time. Thomas and Helmud each took a separate truck and began working feverishly.

"Hurry!" the man shouted anxiously. "There are more trucks coming! We have got to keep working!"

In the midst of his rush to get everything unloaded, Thomas glanced over at the rest of the factory workers. Everyone was doing their job at a frantic pace, trying to keep up with the flow of shoes and laces and boxes that were going in and out, up and down, and all around the room. Slowly, it dawned on Thomas that the harder he worked, the harder everyone else had to work, too.

"I guess we have more work to do."

XXII

Break Time!

At that moment, the loud whistle sounded once again, echoing throughout the city. Immediately, all of the conveyor belts and elevators and equipment stopped operating. Everyone scurried over to their lunchboxes and pulled out identical cups of coffee and small biscuits for their mid-morning break.

Helmud and Thomas stood in place, staring in shock at one another. Thomas wondered to himself how they had gotten so involved in operation of the shoe factory so quickly.

Suddenly, the man reappeared and offered the pair some coffee and biscuits. He looked very rushed and worried about something.

"I'm so glad you are here!" he announced. "We have a lot to do and you are helping make the city run better than ever before. But if we don't continue to work hard, everything will fall apart!"

With that, the man ran off to deal with some other major problem. Thomas sat down against a wall while Helmud stretched out on the floor. They could overhear the other workers chattering as they rested. The only thing the people talked about was how well or poorly they thought work was going that morning.

Thomas turned to Helmud, who was still sprawled out on the floor in exhaustion.

"This is useless," he whispered. "For everything one of them is doing, there is someone else busy undoing it. I don't think anything actually gets done at all – except staying busy and getting tired."

Helmud groaned. He had suspected something like that, but he hadn't been able to figure it out like Thomas had. The hudlunk had been too busy unloading boxes with his teeth to even look around.

Suddenly, the man appeared again, almost as frantic as before. He rubbed his hands together in a worried sort of way, saying, "We start back up in five minutes. I hope you are ready! We need you to keep Macroeconomics running!"

Thomas looked up at the man and inquired, "What's the purpose of all this hard work?"

"Why," the man answered with an incredulous look on his face, "freedom, of course!"

"Freedom?"

"Yes! You see, if we can keep everyone working, then there will be enough things for everybody. And everyone knows that when you have enough, then you are free because you don't need anything else."

"But to do that," the man continued earnestly, "we must all work hard together! Now, the break is almost over. Work hard until lunch and I'll make sure you get a meal even though you didn't sign up for one. After lunch, we will do our jobs until the afternoon break. After break, we will work again until it's time for dinner."

"What happens after dinner?"

"Oh," answered the man, "we will all be very busy at home getting as much done as we can in preparation for tomorrow. It's the only way to stay ahead, you know."

Thomas tried to speak, but the whistle blew again just as he opened his mouth.

"Back to work!" the man shouted as everyone charged to their positions. The conveyor belts, elevators and equipment had already started running again. It was a mad scramble as each person hurried to catch up with the work that was piling up in front of them.

Three trucks drove into the factory at the same time, putting Thomas and Helmud far behind schedule before they had even started. The pair hurried into separate trucks and began unloading them as fast as they could.

The rest of the morning and all afternoon continued at the same frenzied pace. The two friends had no chance to talk the entire time. Even during their breaks, they both just wanted to rest, not have a conversation.

Finally, at dinner time, Thomas commented to Helmud, "This doesn't feel much like freedom to me. I don't have any needs, but I also don't have any time to do what I want. What good is that?"

Helmud nodded in agreement as he ate his food. It was a chewy, bread-like substance with little flavor. He really didn't like it, but it was all that was available. Everyone else was eating the same food and talking about how the production lines had been that day.

The man stopped by again with a slip of paper. "Here," he said. "This is your sleeping room assignment."

Thomas looked at the paper. It read:

Sector F, Building 783, Room 54F, Beds 1 & 2

After dinner, the pair left the factory with all of the other workers. Fortunately, the city was laid out in a large square with all of the labels prominently displayed and in order. So Sector F, Building 783, Room 54F was not that hard to find.

Once they reached their room, Thomas and Helmud were surprised to find two beds, one on each side, a bathroom to share – and two piles of shoes in the middle of the floor.

In front of one bed, the pile was labeled:

Bed #1, Unlacing Pile. Unlace the shoes and place them in the pile beside Bed #2

In front of the other bed, the pile was labeled:

Bed #2, Lacing Pile. Lace the shoes and place them in the pile beside Bed #1

Thomas stared at the two piles and sighed, "I guess we have more work to do."

The two sat down beside their beds with the piles in between them. Helmud took the unlacing pile and began to take the laces out of the shoes with his teeth. It was difficult work, but he soon began to do it quite quickly. As each shoe was unlaced, he tossed it into the pile of shoes in front of Thomas. Then Thomas took the shoes out of that pile and began to lace them up again.

The unlacing seemed to go faster. Soon Thomas saw that his pile was getting bigger, not smaller. He sighed and determined that he would work harder. After half an hour, his pile was growing small again. Just then, the whistle blew one more time and the lights in the room went out. It was finally bed time!

The Whistle

XXIII

The City Falls Apart

The next day, Thomas and Helmud started the same routine all over again. The man scurried by at regular intervals with the same very worried look on his face.

"Hurry! Hurry!" he would say. "If we don't work faster, the city of Macroeconomics will fall apart!"

This went on for three more days, each of them blurring together in a haze of loading and unloading, lacing and unlacing, whistles and unwhistles.

Finally, after another particularly bland lunch, Thomas said to Helmud, "We have to get out of here. We may be very important in keeping the city running, but I don't see why the city should run at all."

"What should we do?" asked Helmud.

Thomas paused, "I think that all we need to do is get up and walk out."

Helmud gasped, "Can we do that? The man said that everything would fall apart."

Thomas thought for a few moments. "Maybe it would be good if everything did stop working. Besides, the city seemed to be doing alright before we got here. It should be able to do fine without us."

Just then, the whistle blew. As they rushed to their positions, Thomas and Helmud decided to think about the idea some more before they did anything rash. As it happened, work was so busy that it wasn't until the end of the day before they had a chance to talk again.

That night, after the lights went out, the two discussed their plan once more. They decided to leave right after lunch the next day. That way, they would have had two meals and there would still be enough sunlight to travel a good distance away from the city.

The next day when they woke up, both of them were determined that this was the day of escape.

After working all morning, Thomas and Helmud were glad when lunchtime finally came. They ate their meal as usual and quietly encouraged each other that they were about to do the right thing. Then, as the whistle blew and everyone rushed to their places, the boy and the hudlunk walked across the factory floor and out through Door 54A of Building 8 in Sector C.

Just as they were leaving, four trucks arrived at the unloading area. Since no one was there to empty them, the drivers began calling for assistance.

Other workers abandoned their positions to help with the crisis. As a result, unlaced shoes ended up in the laced pile; right-footed shoes shot down the wrong chute into the left-footed shoe pile; and boxes were shipped out of the factory completely empty!

Soon, there were problems throughout the city. The empty boxes stymied the workers in the other factories and shut down entire assembly lines. One factory after another quit operating until the city stopped functioning. The lights stopped lighting; the conveyor belts stopped conveying; trucks stopped trucking and workers stopped working. Everything was in such a state of disarray that no one knew how to get it started again.

Over the next few days, the citizens of Macroeconomics were deeply divided. Half of them shouted desperately that the factories needed to start up again immediately. They were sure that this was the worst catastrophe that could have ever happened. The other half of the workers discovered that they now had time to play cards, kick balls and race small cars down the conveyor belts. They didn't think that the factories should ever re-open.

Meanwhile, Thomas and Helmud had successfully escaped the city of Macroeconomics and were walking further and further away. They were very excited to be traveling once again.

"I'll be happy if I never have to lace a shoe again!" Thomas said wearily.

Helmud growled in agreement, "The only thing I liked about that place was the coffee."

As they walked along, the boy decided that being too busy might be just as bad as being too lazy. Neither one gave a person freedom.

Entering the Desert of Fear

XXIV

Desert of Fear

Thomas and Helmud enjoyed the next three days of the journey in peace and contentment. The road they were following skirted along some mountains and crossed a broad plain. The weather was perfect and they found plenty of food along the way.

As the young boy and his hudlunk friend walked along, Thomas thought about how much he enjoyed Helmud's company. He wasn't the scary beast he first seemed to be. In fact, he had become a good friend and companion. It would be sad to say goodbye when they finally finished their journey.

Thomas also thought about how much he missed his family. He wondered if they were worried about him and whether they were out looking for him. Thomas was sure that they would never be able to find him. It was up to him to bring the Lantern of Elsdat to the Land of Freedom if he ever wanted to get home.

As the days passed, the beautiful weather started to change. It was getting hotter and hotter. Thomas had occasionally worn his jacket before, but now it stayed tucked in his backpack with the lantern. Even at night, the temperature didn't drop much at all. As a result, Thomas found it difficult to get a good night's sleep. He tossed and turned, trying to cool down somehow.

"Is summer coming?" Thomas asked Helmud, who had been silent much of the day.

"No," he replied solemnly. "The temperature is getting hotter because we are approaching the Desert of Fear."

"The Desert of Fear?"

"Yes," answered Helmud. "Hudlunk legends say that the Land of Freedom can only be reached by going through the Desert of Fear."

"What is the Desert of Fear?"

"I don't know. It's in the Land of Bondage, but I've never been there. All I know is that it's a horrible place with spiders, rats and other creepy things."

"Yuck," said Thomas. Spiders and rats were disgusting, but they didn't frighten him too much. As he looked at Helmud, though, Thomas could see that spiders, rats and other creepy things frightened the hudlunk a great deal.

"You don't have to keep traveling with me," Thomas told his friend. "I don't want you to have to go to some place that's horrible."

Helmud took a deep breath. "That's okay. I would rather walk through the Desert of Fear with you than go back alone through all of the places we've already been."

Thomas nodded. The hudlunk had a good point.

As the pair continued walking, they finally arrived at the place where the road ended. One forlorn tree marked the end of all vegetation as well. Beyond it, the land was barren and looked completely uninhabitable.

Just past the tree was the start of a trail. It was rocky and poorly cared for. Thomas groaned when he saw it. This wasn't going to be easy. To the side of the trail was an old, collapsed sign that was lying face down on the ground. Helmud flipped it over. It read:

Welcome, my dear
To the Desert of Fear
A place full of nightmares to rattle your bones
They'll make you wish that you'd never left home
Look back at the tree that you have just passed
For this pretty sight shall be your last

Thomas shuddered. Helmud did, too.

The pair briefly exchanged glances and then, in silent agreement, started trudging down the path. After half an hour of walking, the last tree was no longer in sight. Instead, the whole world seemed to be one vast desert of rocks, sandy hills and more rocks. Thomas and Helmud often found themselves stumbling and tripping.

In addition, the weather was getting hotter and drier with every single step. Thomas could feel his lips peeling and Helmud's tongue was now hanging out of his mouth. Even the ground seemed to be getting hotter and hotter. Finally, the pair decided that they had to get a drink and find a place to spend the night.

"Let's climb the next hill and see if there's anything just ahead," Thomas suggested.

Since there was nothing in sight that would make a good shelter, Helmud agreed. Leaning forward, they climbed slowly up the hill. When at last Thomas and Helmud reached the top, they were astonished at the view of the small valley below.

There, beside the path, right in the middle of the rocky desert, stood a house! Not only that, but the building had an adobe wall that enclosed a courtyard with trees growing in it! Thomas hoped that the owner of the house would be kind enough to let them stay for the night. The two hurried down the hill to find out.

As they got closer, Thomas and Helmud saw that the building had a single entrance with an old, wooden sign above it. The sign read:

House of False Safety

Neither of them understood what the sign meant, but Thomas did notice a crude doorbell beside the door.

Motioning to it, he commented, "We might as well try it. There is nowhere else for us to stay tonight."

Helmud nodded. His paws were sore from the rocky trail and he was really thirsty.

When Thomas pulled the cord, a small gong rang inside the house. The noise echoed for several moments, but no one came to the door. The pair waited awkwardly for a couple of minutes. Then, since they had nowhere else to go, they decided to ring the doorbell one more time.

This time the wooden door opened after just a few seconds. Standing in the doorway was a tall, thin man with a thin mustache, thin mouth and even thinner eyes. He wore a short, thin coat and trousers that ended just below his knees. His long, black boots went up his thin legs to where his trousers left off.

The man looked down at Thomas. He smiled a thin smile and said, "Welcome! We have been expecting you."

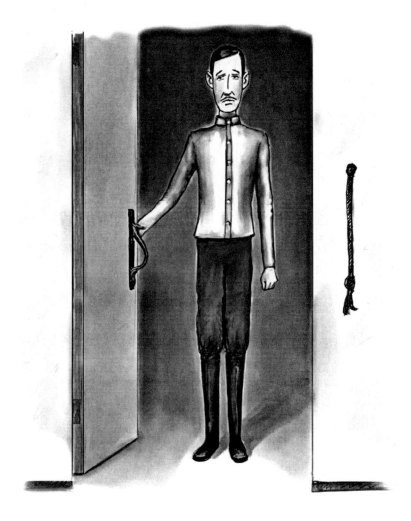

The Thin Man

XXV

House of False Safety

The man stepped back and opened the door wider. As he did, Thomas was amazed to see a lobby and the courtyard beyond it. It was bright and filled with plants. There was a playground and a swimming pool, too. Helmud immediately noticed the large, grassy yard to play on.

A waiter appeared out of nowhere and offered both of them some water.

"Wow!" said Thomas.

"This is amazing," Helmud chimed in.

"It's the House of False Safety," replied the thin man, bowing. "Dinner will be served in fifteen minutes in the dining room. James will show you to your quarters."

The man snapped his fingers and a porter came over.

"Take our guests to room 12," directed the man.

The porter bowed and motioned for the pair to follow him. As they walked, Thomas and Helmud were amazed at how pleasant the temperature was. It was a welcome relief from the hot desert. Thomas also noticed that all of the rooms were numbered.

"This must be a hotel of some sort," he said to Helmud.

After being shown to their room, Thomas and Helmud headed to the dining room for dinner. There appeared to be only one other guest. He was a nervous sort of fellow who said his name was Frank.

The waiters brought Thomas a menu which included all of his favorite foods. He could hardly decide what to eat until he saw the peanut butter and jelly sandwich. He hadn't had one of those since he had left home!

Helmud's menu was full of hudlunk delights and he was overjoyed at the prospect of eating a great meal.

After dinner, Thomas and Helmud decided to explore the hotel some more. They discovered that the pool had a diving board and the playground had swings, ropes and even a ten-foot slide.

That night, as they settled into bed, Thomas and Helmud talked about how nice the hotel was. It seemed like the perfect place to stay and rest before continuing on their journey.

Thomas furrowed his brow. "I'm still worried about a couple of things."

"What are they?"

"Well, I wonder how much this is going to cost us," he replied. "I also wonder how we will pay for it."

Helmud didn't know the answer to that question, so he suggested they ask at the front desk in the morning.

"That's a good idea," replied Thomas.

The boy continued thinking and spoke up once again, saying, "I also wonder what the man meant when he said that they had been expecting us."

Helmud had no answer to that either, mostly because he had fallen sound asleep.

The next morning, Thomas was determined to find out the answers to his questions as soon as possible. On their way to the front desk, though, he and Helmud were invited to breakfast by Frank. Thomas readily agreed, hoping that the other hotel guest would have some useful information to share. The trio sat together in the dining room, looking out over the pool. It was another beautiful day.

"How long have you been here?" asked Thomas.

"Just a little while, maybe a week," replied Frank. "I'm going to the Land of Freedom, but I decided to stop here for a few days before continuing."

"You're going to the Land of Freedom?"

"Yes. I'm tired of living in the Land of Bondage so I decided to risk the journey. No one has ever made it to the Land of Freedom, you know."

"No one?"

"No one," repeated Frank.

Thomas felt a chill of fear so he decided to change the subject. "Why did you choose to stop here?"

Frank looked at him in surprise. "It's safe here," he said. "The journey from here to the Land of Freedom is very scary and very dangerous!"

"Really?"

"Oh, yes. You should see for yourself. Go look at the displays in the museum."

"Museum?"

"Yes," Frank answered. "There is a museum in the basement with a map of the Desert of Fear and exhibits of what lies ahead. You really must go see it. Why, I'm down there at least once a day so that I can study and prepare for the next part of my journey."

Frank shivered a bit, "I'm feeling cold, are you?"

Thomas and Helmud shook their heads. It actually felt just a bit warm to them. A few minutes later, they excused themselves to go to the front desk. Thomas still wanted to find out about the bill. The clerk at the desk wasn't much help, though, so they asked to see the thin man with the thin mustache.

When the man appeared, he smiled broadly at the pair.

"What may I help you with?" he inquired.

"Um, we were wondering how much it costs to stay here," replied Thomas. "We want to be able to pay for our lodging."

The man looked at Thomas in shock. "Pay?" he said. "On no, children can stay here for free. There is nothing to worry about."

Thomas and Helmud exchanged surprised looks. This was better than they had expected!

"One other thing," Thomas continued. "We heard that there is a museum here. Can you show us where it is?"

The man smiled and pointed across the lobby to a small door that was labeled:

The Museum of Fear

"There is no admission charge," he said. "Please feel free to explore it as frequently as you wish. Most of our guests visit several times during their stay."

"Thank you," replied Thomas. "I think we will."

The two travelers proceeded across the lobby. On their way, they passed Frank, who was by now shivering a great deal.

"*I wonder why he's so cold,*" thought Thomas.

Freezing Frank

XXVI

Museum of Fear

The door leading to the Museum of Fear opened easily in Thomas' hand. He and Helmud walked down a flight of stairs and along a short hallway before entering the large room that was the museum. Thomas noticed that the hallway had several unmarked doors on each side.

The museum was just as Frank had described, full of maps and exhibits. Thomas glanced around the room and decided to study the large map of the Desert of Fear. The first place on the map was a long stretch of land which began just outside the House of False Safety. It was labeled:

Spiders and Rats

A sign indicated that the rats were as large as dogs and the spiders were known to stand six feet tall and were very poisonous. Thomas shivered involuntarily as he thought of six-foot spiders.

The three remaining places were labeled in order:

Rejection The Great Chasm The Last House

The place named Rejection was located right after the area called Spiders and Rats. It looked like another stretch of desert and it ended at the Great Chasm. On the other side of the chasm was the Land of Freedom. Right beside the entrance to the Land of Freedom was a small building which was identified as the Last House.

Of all these sites, the Great Chasm was the one that captured Thomas' attention. It appeared to be a large canyon with a narrow bridge over it. Thomas thought that the bridge looked scary. He began to shiver.

"*Maybe the bridge on the map isn't drawn accurately,*" Thomas told himself.

Thomas hoped that there was a big bridge at the chasm. If the bridge was sturdy enough, he thought that he would be able to cross it. The idea of crossing a rickety old bridge terrified Thomas.

Helmud came running up to Thomas, shivering. He had been closely examining the spider exhibit and was full of different scary facts.

"Let's go," Thomas said. "I've seen enough."

Once back in their room, Thomas put on his jacket to warm up. Then the pair decided to go outside and play in the sunshine. Even after an hour, though, they both still felt chilled.

Something about the hotel troubled Thomas, but he was not sure what it was. After enjoying two peanut butter and jelly sandwiches for lunch, Thomas said, "Helmud, I think we should start planning to leave."

"Maybe so," Helmud answered, shivering. "But I'd like to go to the museum at least once more. Frank is right. We should study all we can before we go further."

Thomas reluctantly agreed to one more visit. "I don't know that it will do us much good," he remarked.

As they started back to the museum, Thomas noticed Frank sitting out in the sunshine. He was wrapped in several blankets, but still seemed to be shivering.

Once down the stairs, Helmud hurried to the museum. Thomas wasn't so excited, so he meandered slowly down the hallway, looking at the other doors.

"*I wonder where these all lead,*" Thomas thought. He tried a doorknob and immediately let go of it.

"Ouch!"

The doorknob was so cold that it hurt his hand. "*This must be the door that goes to the hotel's freezer,*" he said to himself.

Just then, there was a sound at the top of the stairs. Thomas stepped into the museum and out of sight.

Peeking back down the hallway, he saw the thin man and a waiter come down the stairs, carrying a bundle of blankets. It was Frank! Thomas watched as they opened the door to the freezer and put Frank's body inside.

Thomas stayed hidden until the thin man and the waiter had gone back upstairs. Then, rushing to Helmud, he told him about what he had seen.

"We have to go look in the freezer!" he exclaimed.

Helmud hesitantly agreed and the pair snuck cautiously down the hallway. Using a cloth to protect his hand, Thomas opened the freezer door. As he did, the two companions were shocked to discover a large room that was filled with frozen people. Frank was there, too, already frozen solid!

Slamming the door shut, Thomas turned to Helmud and instructed him, "Pretend that nothing has happened. We need to get back to our room."

Helmud nodded in agreement. He was so cold now that his teeth were chattering.

In their room, Thomas and Helmud tried to understand what they had just seen. At first, they thought that the people had been put into the freezer and then frozen. But that made no sense to Thomas. Frank was already shivering before they put him in the freezer.

Then Thomas had an idea. "Helmud! I think I know the answer! Maybe this freezer isn't like a regular freezer. Maybe the people aren't frozen because they are in the freezer. I'll bet that the freezer is frozen because frozen people are put in it."

Helmud cocked his head to one side, trying hard to understand what Thomas was saying.

"Then how did the people get frozen?" he asked, still uncertain of what Thomas was saying.

"Look at how you have been getting colder the longer we stay here," Thomas said slowly. "I think that all of those people were frozen by fear."

Helmud's eyes widened. He suddenly realized that if they choose to stay at the House of False Safety much longer, they, too, could end up frozen forever.

"We have got to get out of here!" Helmud growled. "Right away!"

Thomas agreed and grabbed his backpack. Then he and Helmud headed out of their room, through the lobby and toward the front door of the hotel. The thin man stopped them right at the door before they could leave.

"What are you doing?" he asked suspiciously.

"It's time for us to leave," answered Thomas politely.

The thin man looked closely at him and then bowed as he stepped aside. "Very well," he said. "It has been our pleasure to have you staying here with us. Please come back again soon."

With that, the man opened the door to let Thomas and Helmud out. A blast of hot air hit them in the face.

"Will you be returning home or continuing through the Desert of Fear?" the man inquired politely.

"We are going to the Land of Freedom," Thomas replied resolutely.

"Good luck," the thin man replied, bowing once again. "Please say 'Hi' to the spiders for me."

Helmud shivered at that remark.

A Huge Rat

XXVII

The Journey Continues

"Do we really have to go through the Desert of Fear?" Helmud pleaded as they left the House of False Safety.

"I'm afraid so," answered Thomas as he put his jacket in his backpack. He felt sorry for his friend. "You don't have to come if you don't want to."

Helmud thought about it for a little while. He wasn't so sure that he was willing to go further, but there was nothing for him to go back to, either.

Finally, he said, "I'm coming with you. But let's hurry."

As he spoke, the hudlunk stopped shivering.

They hiked out of the valley and back onto the rocky plain. The ground was hot and a dry desert wind whirled all around them. Every now and then, Helmud thought he heard a noise. The first time, he shrieked for fear that a rat or a spider was about to attack them.

"We need to get out of here before it gets dark," Helmud said fearfully. "I don't think I can stay here overnight."

Thomas agreed. The place felt creepy to him, too.

The journey continued peacefully for a while. Suddenly, though, Helmud spotted a spider. It was a hundred yards off the path and, just as the museum had warned, it was huge. The hudlunk shrieked and hid behind Thomas.

Thomas examined the spider while Helmud crouched behind him, begging to run away. Within seconds, even more spiders appeared. Soon there was a wall of spiders blocking their way! While Helmud huddled in fright, Thomas' thoughts raced, trying to figure out what to do.

The spiders were gray-green, with six foot long legs, and round, speckled bodies. To Thomas, they looked like overgrown daddy-long-legs, although their fangs made them look very menacing. However, the boy couldn't tell if they were dangerous or not.

On top of that, Helmud was pawing at Thomas, begging to run away.

"Helmud," Thomas said. "Tell me this: What do you think is the scariest creature I have ever met?"

"I don't know," Helmud answered fearfully.

"It was you!"

"What?"

"Remember when you and I first met in the forest? You were roaring so loudly that I thought you were going to eat me. Boy was I wrong! Maybe these spiders are like that, too. They could be scary, but not at all dangerous."

"Do you really think so?"

"Well," Thomas continued. "We need to be careful, but let's not be afraid until we know there is a reason."

By now, the spiders had approached within thirty feet of them. They towered over the pair and blocked the path. The spiders stared at Thomas and Helmud with their beady red eyes, but they didn't come any closer. It was then that Thomas noticed the large piles of white objects behind the spiders.

"Look!" he exclaimed to Helmud. "Those are their eggs! I'll bet that the spiders are only trying to protect them. If we stay away from their eggs, the spiders probably won't even bother us."

"I sure hope you're right," whimpered Helmud.

Slowly, the pair walked in a wide arc around the spiders' eggs. As they did, the spiders stayed between the two intruders and their treasure. They didn't approach or attack Thomas and Helmud at all.

After making their detour, the pair got back on the trail and continued walking. Thomas glanced back and saw that the spiders were moving back to their positions to watch for any further intruders.

"Whew," croaked Helmud. "That was a close! I wonder where the rats are?"

"There might not be any rats," Thomas replied hopefully. "The museum map could have been wrong."

Just as Thomas closed his mouth, though, a huge rat appeared in front of them, walking on its hind legs. It startled Helmud so much that he let out a loud shriek.

Waves of fear washed over Thomas. This rat was as big as a large dog and it had very sharp teeth. Thomas had heard lots of stories about rats at home and he didn't want to have to fight one this size. However, even though Helmud was starting to back away, Thomas resolved to stand his ground, at least for the moment.

They were not prepared for what happened next. Instead of attacking them, the rat cocked its head to one side and looked quizzically at the newcomers cowering in front of him.

Then, the rat opened its mouth and asked in a very pleasant voice, "May I help you?"

Thomas and Helmud looked at the rat and then each other in shock.

"May you do what?" Thomas asked uncertainly.

"May I help you?" repeated the rat politely. "I am Simon Ratticus. Is there anything I can do for you?"

"Don't eat us!" yelped Helmud, still shaking in fear.

Simon chuckled. "Don't worry, I'm a vegetarian."

The boy breathed a sigh of relief, but Helmud eyed the rat very skeptically. "Where in the world do you get vegetables out here?" he asked.

"From my garden, silly," the rat replied. "Come along. I'll show you."

Thomas and Helmud watched the rat as he began to walk down the path.

"I can't think of any better ideas, can you?" Thomas whispered.

Looking back toward the spiders, Helmud said quietly, "I guess not."

Simon had already gone a little ways ahead, so it took a minute for the two to catch up with him.

"We grow our vegetables underground," the rat said nonchalantly. "There are natural springs in the caverns and that's where we have our gardens."

"What about sunlight?" Thomas asked.

We get plenty of that from the cave openings," Simon replied. "That and our light bulbs."

"Light bulbs?" Thomas asked incredulously.

"Of course," answered Simon. "Who do you think invented them in the first place?"

"Bless my whiskers," Simon continued, bending down to pick something up. "I almost forgot my book."

"Your book?" asked Thomas in disbelief.

"Yes. I was outside doing a little research before you came along. I was reading a very thorough study on the thermodynamic properties of geological formations from the Mesozoic period. I am hoping that it will help us improve our underground cooling system."

Thomas and Helmud looked at each other in amazement.

"So," continued Simon, "where are you two going? We get very few travelers through here, you know."

"You dropped your gum on the floor and ruined the carpet."

XXVIII

Spires of Rejection

After reaching Simon's cave, the trio shared a dinner of carrots and radishes. The food wasn't exactly what either Thomas or Helmud would have chosen, but they were thankful nonetheless. As they ate, Thomas and Helmud explained about their journey to the Land of Freedom.

"Yes," nodded Simon, "I've heard of such a place. Every once in a great while, someone comes through here looking for the Land of Freedom. But no one has ever returned to say that they had reached it."

Simon continued, "Perhaps they made it and decided to stay or maybe something horrible happened. I, myself, have never traveled very far in that direction. I am sorry that I can't be more helpful."

"You have been very helpful to us already," said Thomas, "and the food was wonderful."

"Thank you," Simon answered graciously. "You are most welcome to spend the night."

Thomas and Helmud were happy to accept his offer. It seemed much safer to spend the night in Simon's cave than above ground.

Following a tour of Simon's vegetable gardens, the two bedded down for the night in Mr. Ratticus' guest room. The next morning, after a pleasantly crunchy breakfast of more carrots and radishes, the pair politely excused themselves.

"Mr. Ratticus, I do think that we must be on our way now," Thomas said. "Thank you for your hospitality. You have been a very gracious host."

"Yes," agreed Helmud, who had never quite gotten used to the idea of a friendly, dog-sized rat. "I'm sorry that I roared at you."

"I am delighted to have met you both," Simon said pleasantly. "Before you go, here is some food and let me give you some advice for the journey ahead. Do just as I say and you will be able to reach the Land of Freedom."

Thomas listened intently.

"Follow this path as far as possible. It will run alongside a canyon and eventually reach the bridge that goes over the part of the canyon that is called the Great Chasm. Be warned: There will be opportunities to turn off the path. Do not take them. They will only bring you misery. Take care, my friends."

Simon stood waving to them as they left.

"Good bye!" Thomas called back as he and Helmud resumed their journey.

Their hike along the path continued quite smoothly. The ground was still rocky, but it was beginning to level out. Even better, the desert wind had stopped blowing. Every now and then, a rat appeared in the distance, causing Helmud to jump, but nothing bad happened. The journey was, in fact, becoming quite pleasant.

As time passed, the path brought them along the edge of the canyon Simon had mentioned. Its sides dropped off in a gradual slope. Every so often, a trail would break off to the left, descending to the canyon floor. As they walked, Thomas began to see some trees, a bit of grass and a narrow stream down below. Up on the rim, it was still fairly desolate.

After a couple of hours had passed, Helmud nudged Thomas and pointed off to the horizon. The path ahead veered further out from the canyon. In the distance, Thomas could see that it was taking them right through a group of tall earthen spires. Helmud thought that there was something perched on top of each spire. He lifted his nose and sniffed the air for a few moments.

"You see those things on top?" the hudlunk pointed with his paw. "They're people!"

"That's funny," Thomas shrugged, "I wonder what they are doing up there?"

"I don't know," said Helmud, "but let's be careful."

"What could people sitting on top of pillars do to us?" Thomas pondered out loud.

Soon, the pair found themselves approaching the spires. The pillars were made out of mud and rocks and stood over 10 feet high. The path went directly down the middle of all of the spires.

The two travelers saw that each spire did, indeed, have a person sitting on top of it. This fact didn't bother the hudlunk very much, but as they got closer, Thomas started getting more nervous and upset.

"What's the matter?" Helmud asked.

"I know all of the people on those spires," Thomas replied fearfully, "and none of them like me."

"What do you mean?" the hudlunk asked. It seemed to him that there was nothing un-likeable about Thomas.

Before the boy could reply, the school janitor, who was sitting on top of the first spire, spoke out, "Thomas, you dropped your gum on the floor and ruined the carpet in your third grade classroom! Shame on you!"

Thomas covered his head. He had hoped that nobody had seen him when that happened.

The next person, a former babysitter, looked at Thomas and announced, "You took a piece of candy from your little sister when she wasn't looking. You thief!"

A teacher joined the chorus. "You didn't do your math homework and lied to me about it."

Next, one of the bullies at school started calling Thomas a coward. "You ran away from me because you're a chicken!" he declared.

Then, the bully flapped his arms and imitated a chicken, saying, "Brawk! Brawk!"

Thomas was feeling totally humiliated. It was all he could do to not run away. He figured there were at least 100 more people waiting to accuse and embarrass him.

Just then, Thomas noticed a trail that led away from the spires and down to the canyon floor.

"Let's go that way instead," he urged Helmud.

"I think we ought to stay on the path like we were told to by Simon," Helmud answered firmly.

"Come on!" Thomas urged. "We can go around the rest of these people and get back on the path later."

The hudlunk refused to budge.

Thomas shouted, "We have to get off this path!"

He was very afraid of what else these people might know. They might tell about the night he wet his bed or when he cheated on that test in school last week.

Helmud refused to budge. "Simon says go straight," he replied. "That's what we need to do."

Thomas argued with his friend for several minutes. All the while, the people on the earthen spires chastised him about incidents from his past. Soon, they began to humiliate the boy concerning his behavior while on this journey – even for how he had treated Helmud.

The hudlunk continued to stand his ground as Thomas begged, "You hear what they are saying! I can't listen to this anymore!" Finally, the boy declared in desperation, "Well, I'm going to take the shortcut by myself then!"

At that, Helmud stepped in front of Thomas and blocked his path. "You are my friend," he said to Thomas. "We are going to stay together and we are going to go the right way."

Thomas looked at Helmud in dismay.

Helmud continued, "I don't expect you to be perfect and I don't care what all of these people say about you. You are my friend and you will always be my friend."

Thomas could tell by looking in the hudlunk's eyes that Helmud meant every word he said.

"Okay," he finally acquiesced. "I will stay on the path."

"You can ride on my back and plug your ears, if that will help."

"No," Thomas replied. "I'll walk."

Thomas started down the path once more. The people on the spires called out all kinds of embarrassing and even dreadful secrets about him, but the boy continued to go forward. At times, he covered his head in shame at what was said. All the while, though, Helmud walked right beside Thomas with his head held high.

"I am proud to have a friend like you," Helmud kept saying over and over.

Finally, after a withering two hour journey, they left the spires behind them. There were no longer any trails descending off to the side. There was only the main path which climbed up a steep hill just ahead.

"Let's stop at the top and eat lunch," suggested Thomas.

"That sounds like a good idea," Helmud replied.

The food that Simon Ratticus had given them consisted of more carrots and radishes, but that was better than nothing. And Thomas was hungry enough that even radishes sounded good to eat. Wearily, the boy shifted his backpack on his shoulders and the two trudged up the incline together.

When Thomas and Helmud finally reached the top of the hill, the view was so majestic that it took Helmud's breath away. In front of them lay a vast canyon, which was none other than the Great Chasm.

Sunlight reflected off the canyon walls in a myriad of directions, creating a mosaic of red, brown and even blue hues that danced before their eyes. It was the most amazing sight Helmud had ever seen.

On the other side of the chasm there was a fertile land with lush fields and forests and all kinds of people and animals. There was even a beautiful, blue city on a hill in the distance. The entrance to this land was just a short hike from the far edge of the chasm. At the entrance, there was an archway with a sign which read:

Welcome to the Land of Freedom

The Great Chasm

XXIX

The Great Chasm

When Helmud realized that they had reached the Great Chasm, he began prancing about in excitement. They were almost there! He was hardly able to contain his joy.

To the hudlunk's amazement, though, Thomas didn't appear to be excited at all. In fact, he seemed quite discouraged – even to the point of giving up.

"What's wrong?" Helmud asked. "We're almost there!"

"Maybe so. But look at what's between here and there," Thomas replied fearfully.

Helmud followed the trail with his eyes. It went down the hill to the bridge that crossed over the chasm. On the other side of the chasm was a small, weather beaten old shack. It stood by the entrance to the Land of Freedom.

"Well," said Helmud with a note of confusion in his voice, "I see a bridge and a house. No big deal."

"No big deal!" Thomas almost shouted at Helmud. "You call that bridge no big deal?"

Helmud examined it more closely. It was a very narrow rope suspension bridge that had wooden slats for a walkway. It didn't look very sturdy, but at least there were ropes on each side for hand rails.

"Do you see how rickety that bridge is?" Thomas asked.

Helmud nodded.

"Do you see how far we will fall if the bridge breaks?"

Helmud nodded again. It was quite a distance down to the floor of the canyon. If the bridge broke, they would certainly not survive the fall.

Suddenly, Helmud remembered Thomas' behavior at the Stream of Apathy and he began to understand.

"Are you afraid of bridges?" he asked.

Thomas' face grew pale with fear. "I hate them. I won't go near one unless it's really sturdy."

"Why?" Helmud asked. He couldn't imagine how a boy who was so brave around spiders could be so scared of bridges.

Thomas bit his lip and looked down. "My right foot got caught in a rope bridge at scout camp once and I fell off the side. I won't even cross the little bridges on the school playground anymore. I'm terrified of any bridge that moves when I'm on it."

Helmud wasn't sure what a scout camp was, but he knew that getting a paw caught in anything was a very serious matter.

"Do you want to go back down the hill for a few minutes?" the hudlunk suggested, "Maybe if you didn't look at the bridge, you wouldn't be so frightened."

Thomas shook his head. He had a good memory and a vivid imagination. He didn't think that being out of sight of the bridge would help much.

"Well," offered Helmud, "in that case, let's walk down to the chasm and get a closer look at the bridge. Maybe it isn't as bad as it seems."

Thomas relented and the two hiked down the hill until they got close to the chasm. Helmud sighed. The bridge was in even worse condition than they had first thought. The ropes were frayed and many of the wooden slats were missing. He even began to get a little nervous.

Thomas stood, frozen in place, shaking. He was more than thirty feet away from the bridge, but he couldn't bring himself to come any closer.

"But the Land of Freedom is right over there," Helmud implored. "You must go on!"

Thomas refused.

"Look at all you have accomplished already!" Helmud continued. "You escaped from Everything City and Lawful Loch Lomen. You made it past the Ladders of Success and the City of Bitterness. We got through the Wasteland of Denial and you rescued me from the mud pits in Hopeless Hollow. We got out of Rooval's maze. I saved you at the Stream of Apathy. We even escaped from the shoe factory in the City of Macroeconomics!"

Helmud continued as enthusiastically as he could, "We left the House of False Safety, and survived spiders and rats, and the spires of rejection!"

"This is all we have left! If we can cross this bridge, we'll reach the Land of Freedom. Then you will be able to go home!"

Nothing Helmud said convinced Thomas even a little bit. The boy was so terrified by the bridge that he was unable to move forward.

Finally, the hudlunk suggested, "What if I go across the bridge first? If I make it across, then I can return to this side and give you a ride on my back. That way, you will already know the bridge is safe. All that you'll have to do is close your eyes and hang on."

Thomas thought about Helmud's idea for a long time. He didn't like it at all, but, try as he might, Thomas couldn't think of a better plan. He knew that he had to get to the Land of Freedom and he also knew that there was no other way to get there.

"Okay," he finally relented. "You try going over first. I'll wait here."

Helmud bounded up and down with joy! Beaming, he said, "I'll hurry over as quickly as I can. Then I'll come back to bring you with me."

The hudlunk turned and approached the bridge. First, he carefully sniffed the ropes. As he did, his stomach started to feel a bit queasy. This didn't look good at all! The ropes smelled old and musty, and the boards were weathered and cracked in many places.

As Helmud put his paw on the first board, the whole bridge groaned under the added weight. Thomas muffled a scream of terror at the sound and ran further away. Still, Helmud continued on. With each new step, the bridge groaned and creaked even more. Every now and then, a board would threaten to break under his weight, but Helmud kept going.

Suddenly, when the hudlunk was half way across, there was a loud crack. A wooden slat had split in two and plummeted to the rocks far below. Helmud sprawled flat on his stomach. Slowly, he pulled himself back up and continued the crossing.

All in all, it only took about three minutes for Helmud to make it across, but it seemed like an eternity to Thomas. When the hudlunk finally arrived on the other side, he placed all four paws on firm ground again and rested for a little while. Just ahead was the archway leading into the Land of Freedom. For a second, Helmud considered exploring a bit, but he decided to save the adventure until Thomas was with him.

The return trip wasn't quite as harrowing as the first crossing. Helmud was used to the groaning and swaying of the bridge, so he was able to move more quickly. Once back on the other side, the hudlunk bounded over to Thomas, full of excitement.

"See?" he cheered. "We can do it! We can make it to the Land of Freedom!"

Crossing the Chasm

XXX

The Crossing

Thomas was still not sure about crossing the bridge. While Helmud was gone, he had been able to sit and think a lot more.

"I don't know," he told Helmud. "Maybe I should just go back to where I started. Maybe the wizard will still let me go home. After all, I tried really hard."

Helmud snorted. "I don't think the wizard will allow that! Why would he send you on this dangerous journey if he was only going to rescue you anyway?"

The hudlunk continued, "The wizard said that you had to bring the Lantern of Elsdat into the Land of Freedom, didn't he? I don't think you're supposed to turn around when you're almost there."

Thomas paused for a while. "Maybe we should just spend the night here and think about it some more."

Helmud growled. He remembered the people in the freezer at the House of False Safety. Waiting around hadn't helped them at all. In fact, it seemed to Helmud that the longer you avoided your fears, the harder it was to finally face them. The hudlunk's mind was made up. Swiftly, he jumped behind Thomas and clamped his teeth onto the back of the boy's shirt collar.

"Ouch! What are you doing?" Thomas protested.

Helmud growled as he gripped the boy firmly. "You are crossing this bridge with me. Either I'll haul you over this way or you can ride on my back as we had planned. But we are going to cross this bridge right now."

Thomas felt himself being dragged toward the bridge. Kicking and fighting did little good. The hudlunk was determined to get Thomas across the chasm – even if he did have to drag him.

As they neared the bridge, Thomas realized that their chances of success would be greater if he cooperated and rode on Helmud's back.

"Okay," he finally surrendered. "I'll ride on your back."

Helmud released his grasp and Thomas collapsed to the ground.

"Strap your backpack on as tightly as possible," Helmud instructed. "I don't want us to drop the lantern after all we've gone through."

Once Thomas' backpack was on, Helmud faced away from the chasm so that the boy could climb on his back without having to stare at the bridge.

"Hold on tight. I don't want you slipping off, either."

Thomas closed his eyes as Helmud began to walk

toward the chasm. The boy cringed in fear as they took their first step onto the rickety bridge.

The ropes groaned and cried out in Thomas' ear. It was as if he could hear them mocking him, saying, "*You will fall and die! You will fall and die!*"

The boy clung tighter to his friend as the pair lurched from board to board. He kept his eyes shut so tight that his face began to hurt.

Suddenly, a board began to break under their weight. The loud cracking noise terrified Thomas and caused Helmud to lunge forward. This dramatic shift in weight made the next board begin to crack as well. Again, the hudlunk moved quickly ahead. Thomas clutched on to his friend's fur as tightly as possible.

More boards began to crack. It was clear to Helmud that the combined weight of both he and Thomas was too much for the weak bridge. Cracking boards were a great concern, but he was even more worried about a rope breaking. Sure enough, a moment later, Helmud felt one of the two ropes holding the walkway snap in two.

Immediately, the floor gave way beneath them. Helmud was suspended in midair, barely hanging on by the handrail ropes while Thomas desperately clung to him. The hudlunk clawed with his back paws, trying to grasp the one remaining floor rope.

After what felt like an eternity, Helmud regained his footing and continued forward. His progress was slow, but he was urged on by the screaming of the ropes as they strained under the weight of the two companions.

All the while, Thomas clung to his friend, eyes closed, so frightened that he could hardly breathe. At one point in the crossing, though, Thomas realized the great risk and sacrifice Helmud was making on his behalf. For a moment, gratitude replaced fear in his heart.

Step after grueling step, Helmud continued across the shaky bridge until he finally reached the other side. With a deep sigh of relief, he grasped the poles that anchored the bridge, and pulled himself and Thomas onto solid ground. Looking back, Helmud saw the bridge dangling by just three ropes. Every few seconds, a board would break loose and fall to the bottom of the chasm.

Moving away from the edge of the chasm, Helmud lay down, chest heaving. Between breaths, he said, "We made it! It's alright now. You can get off."

Thomas slowly opened his eyes. Still trembling from the crossing, he rolled off his friend's back and onto the ground. His heart was pounding and he felt dazed. It was as if his strength was completely gone.

"We made it, Helmud," he managed to say weakly.

The hudlunk lay sprawled on his stomach.

"Yes, we did," he growled back softly.

The pair lay on the ground for several minutes as they recovered from their ordeal. Finally, Thomas lifted his head to look around. As he glanced at the bridge, he realized what a close call they had just had.

"Thank you," Thomas said humbly. "I can never repay you for what you did just now."

"That's okay," his weary companion replied. Helmud barely lifted up his paw and pointed, saying, "See how close we are now?"

There, just beyond them, was the beautiful archway announcing:

Welcome to the Land of Freedom

Beside the archway stood the Last House, an old rundown shack if there ever was one. It reminded Thomas of Henry and Tina's house in the Land of Denial.

Now that their goal was in sight, Thomas felt his hope rising. He realized just how much he missed his family and he could hardly wait to go home. But, seeing that Helmud needed a few more minutes to rest, Thomas continued to sit patiently beside his friend.

"Helmud," said Thomas, "I hope that there is something good for you at the end of this journey."

"I hope so, too," said Helmud. "But it will be wonderful just to see you reach the Land of Freedom."

"Not so fast."

XXXI

The Last House

Finally, Helmud slowly got up and shook himself all over. His muscles ached! Looking back at the bridge, he said, "If we ever need to go back, let's find a different route."

Thomas laughed and stood up, too. Turning toward the archway, the pair smiled and began to walk the last fifty feet into the Land of Freedom. Thomas almost broke out in a run. It looked so warm and inviting!

Before they could pass under the archway, the two friends had to walk past the Last House. Just as they were taking their final steps, though, they heard a noise to their right.

"Not so fast," announced the thin man from the House of False Safety. He stepped out of the Last House, stuck his cane in front of the two travelers, and stopped them from going through the archway. Thomas and Helmud looked at the thin man in astonishment.

"*How did he get here?*" thought Thomas.

The thin man twisted his thin mustache. He stared at them with eyes so cold and cunning that both Helmud and Thomas shuddered. Thomas tried to step forward.

"Not so fast," the man repeated even more firmly. "I am afraid you can't enter the Land of Freedom just yet."

Thomas tried once more to move forward, but the thin man's cane somehow held him back. The man narrowed his eyes and looked at Thomas with an evil glare.

"I am the ruler of the Land of Bondage," he announced with cruel deliberation. "That means that I am also the gatekeeper to the Land of Freedom. I decide who may enter the Land of Freedom and who may not."

"But the wizard said . . ." Thomas interjected.

"Bah!" scoffed the thin man. "The wizard has no power over me! This is my domain and I do as I please."

"Then let us go!" Thomas demanded.

Again, the thin man sneered, "Not so fast. No one may enter the Land of Freedom unless all of their debts are paid. If a creature owes anything at all, then he is forbidden to enter."

Thomas' thoughts raced. Did he owe any money? Was he in trouble for destroying Macroeconomics? Maybe they wanted him to pay to rebuild the city.

Maybe Thaddeus Thudge had gotten free and wanted Thomas to pay for his meal. Perhaps they changed their mind at Lawful Loch Lomen and wanted to send him back to jail.

Thomas decided that whatever the debt was, if he knew the amount, then maybe he could find a way to pay it.

"How much do I owe?" Thomas asked the thin man.

"Let me see," the man casually replied. He opened a large, dusty ledger book that had been tucked under his arm and began flipping its pages.

"Hmmm," he said, "hmmm."

Thomas and Helmud waited in anticipation.

"Well," the thin man finally replied. "It looks as if you don't owe anything, young man. You are free to go."

Thomas got very excited! They were free!

"Let's go!" he exclaimed to Helmud.

The pair surged forward only to be stopped as the thin man's cane came down quickly in front of them once more. Only this time, it blocked Helmud, not Thomas.

"Not so fast," he announced again. "I said that the boy could go into the Land of Freedom. I did not say that the hudlunk could."

"What do you mean?" responded Thomas angrily.

"I mean," said the thin man, sneering, "that your friend is not allowed into the Land of Freedom."

"Why not?" demanded Thomas.

"Because," the thin man answered condescendingly, "all of your debts are paid, but all of his aren't."

"I don't understand," said Thomas.

"It's recorded right here in my ledger book that this creature of yours ate three meals and spent the night at the House of False Safety without paying. Until his debt is paid, he cannot go in."

"That's not true," Helmud spoke up for the first time. "You told us that we could stay for free."

"No," the man sneered once more. "I told you that children could stay for free. I never said anything about hudlunks."

"What?" exclaimed Thomas.

"Just what I said," the thin man declared with a sinister smile. "Children can stay for free at the House of False Safety, but all others must pay."

Helmud bowed his head in such discouragement that Thomas could even feel his friend's despair.

"What will it cost to pay Helmud's debt?"

The thin man looked at his ledger. "25 gondols for the room. 3 gondols for breakfast. Dinner and lunch were 4 gondols each. That's 36 gondols."

The thin man looked down at Thomas and Helmud in obvious satisfaction.

"What if we don't have any gondols?" Thomas asked, hoping that they could somehow work the debt off.

"Then your friend cannot come in."

Thomas pointed at the Last House. "I think that your house could use some work. We could paint it for you."

The thin man laughed cruelly. "No," he said. "Painting the Last House will certainly not do!"

"Then what happens now?" Thomas asked.

The thin man looked at Thomas in evil delight. "You may go into the Land of Freedom. The hudlunk must go back to the House of False Safety with me."

"What will happen to him there?" Thomas asked.

The thin man smiled a deliciously evil smile. He even smacked his lips as he answered Thomas' question.

"I'm not sure, but I think I will put him in the freezer to stay with Frank and all the rest of those fools forever!"

Thomas and Helmud looked horrified at the thought.

"Unless," the thin man continued slyly, "you happen to have something else of value that you could use to pay the hudlunk's debt."

"What about this?"

XXXII

A Final Bid for Freedom

Thomas looked at the thin man in desperation. The man stared back at the boy so coldly that Thomas knew he was quite serious. Helmud hung his head down low.

"Don't worry, Helmud," whispered Thomas. "We will find a way to get you out of this."

"I don't think so," mourned the hudlunk.

"There has to be a way!" Thomas declared.

The two friends stood still for a few moments, unsure of what to do. Suddenly, Thomas' face lit up.

"I might have something I can give you to pay my friend's debt!" he told the thin man.

"Is that so?" replied the man. "I suppose that depends on what it is, doesn't it?"

Thomas reached into his backpack and pulled out the Lantern of Elsdat. He held it out in front of the thin man.

"What about this?" he asked.

The thin man's eyes widened slightly while Helmud gasped in shock.

"No, Thomas, No!" said the hudlunk. "You have to bring the lantern to the Land of Freedom! Don't give it to him!"

The thin man swiftly took the lantern from Thomas and held it up for a better look.

"The Lantern of Elsdat, you say? I have heard of such a lantern. How can I be sure that this is it?"

"Because it is," Thomas answered. "The wizard told me so." Hurriedly, he explained the story of the wizard and the lantern to the thin man. All the while, Helmud was whimpering and begging Thomas not to give it away.

"So, this belonged to a wizard, did it?" the man mused slyly. "I think it may be worth far more than 36 gondols to this wizard you speak of."

"You take it," answered Thomas firmly, putting his arm around Helmud's shoulder.

"So be it!" the thin man declared with a look of great glee. He held the lantern high aloft and began to prance about, laughing. It was the most evil and malicious laugh that Thomas had ever heard.

"I finally have it!" he cackled. "The Lantern of Elsdat is mine!"

"With this lantern," the man continued, "I now have the power to reign over the Land of Freedom and the Land of Bondage!"

Sneering at Thomas, he continued, "Did you really think I would let you into the Land of Freedom? You will never pass through that archway! Now I will throw both of you side-by-side into the freezer forever!"

Thomas and Helmud exchanged looks of utter despair. Everything they had tried to accomplish was lost. Thomas was never going to go home, and he and Helmud would be frozen forever. Helmud began to sob.

Thomas' eyes welled up with tears, too. He turned to Helmud and said quietly, "I'm sorry my idea didn't work. But don't be upset for me. It was worth it to try to free you."

The thin man, overhearing Thomas, laughed again in evil delight. "You fool!" he said. "You lost everything to save an ugly hudlunk!"

Suddenly, the air was filled with a strange sensation like electricity. Everything took on an eerie glow and Helmud's fur stood on end. Then, in a blinding flash, the Wizard of Freedom appeared. He towered over the thin man and stared at him with piercing eyes.

"What do you want? Go away! You have no right to be here!" the thin man cried.

"Oh, yes, I do," the wizard answered in a voice that resounded with power and authority.

"No," whined the man, fiercely clutching the lantern.

"I own the Lantern of Elsdat," the thin man continued. "The Tablets of Elsdat say that the owner of the lantern shall reign over the Land of Freedom! So you are no longer the ruler of the Land of Freedom. I am now ruler over both the Land of Bondage and the Land of Freedom! Go away!"

The wizard laughed. "I believe that the Lantern of Elsdat still belongs to me," he said. "You deceived the boy so the lantern is not rightfully yours."

"You can't have it! It's mine," the thin man retorted. He gripped the lantern tightly to his chest.

The wizard laughed again. "You fool! Do you not see that freedom has come to the Land of Bondage? Your greed has made it possible for the lantern-bearer to fulfill his destiny and has caused you to destroy your own kingdom!"

With a slight wave of his staff, the wizard caused the Lantern of Elsdat to fly out of the thin man's hands and into his own.

"Have you forgotten the legends inscribed on the stone tablets?" the wizard scolded the thin man.

Then the wizard quoted from the ancient words written on the Tablets of Elsdat, "When the lantern-bearer frees himself from bondage, but then chooses bondage again as an act of love, it is then that freedom shall be proclaimed in all the land."

Staring sternly at the thin man, the wizard continued in a booming voice, "Your days are now numbered. Soon freedom will be proclaimed throughout the Land of Bondage. Then it shall once again be known as the Land of Beauty and all of its captives will be set free."

The thin man tried to snatch the lantern back, but the wizard overpowered him with a mere wave of his hand.

"You see?" said the wizard. "The lantern truly does belong with me. Your evil plan to steal it only served to fulfill the words on the tablets. In trying to steal my domain, you have lost your own instead."

The thin man screamed in anger. As he did, his shape began to change before their eyes. In just a matter of seconds, Thomas saw the man turn into the bug at Everything City, Mayor Mingle, Thaddeus Thudge, Mr. Smith in the City of Bitterness, Henry in the Wasteland of Denial, the man in the mud pit, the worried man in Macroeconomics, Mr. Rooval and then back into the thin man.

A few seconds later, the thin man began shrinking and turned into a small, brown cockroach. He let out one last screechy noise and scurried quickly away under the floor boards of the Last House.

"Come with me!" the wizard invited, motioning to the pair. Thomas and Helmud hugged each other in delight. Then, following the wizard, they passed under the archway and into the Land of Freedom at last!

Helmud Wearing the Lantern

XXXIII

Going Home

"I don't understand," Thomas said to the wizard. They were sitting at a table just inside the Land of Freedom.

"What don't you understand?" the wizard replied in a gentle voice.

Thomas had a very confused look on his face. "I'm not sure that I understand anything," he replied.

The wizard laughed. It was a solid laugh, filled with joy.

"My child," he answered, looking kindly at Thomas. "Centuries ago, there was a curse put on the Land of Beauty. That curse removed love from the land. When love was taken away, freedom was also lost because it is love that sets our hearts free. That is how the Land of Beauty became the Land of Bondage."

"You made a choice of love today. You chose to help your friend, Helmud, at great cost to yourself. Because you were the lantern-bearer, that act of love has broken the curse over the Land of Bondage. Now, all people will be able to discover love once again."

"As they do," the wizard continued, "They will find that the Land of Freedom will spring up right where they are. You see, a person doesn't need to go to the Land of Freedom to be free. When you love, wherever you are becomes the Land of Freedom."

Motioning to Thomas and Helmud, the wizard said, "Come. Let me show you."

Soon, all three stood looking across the chasm.

"It looks different," said Helmud in a puzzled voice.

"Yes," replied the wizard contentedly. "It does."

"What is it?" asked Thomas.

"Love has arrived, and with it, freedom," replied the wizard. "It's making the whole land brighter."

All three marveled at the view for a few moments. Then, the wizard turned his fiery eyes on Thomas and Helmud.

"You two," he said solemnly, "have completed the task set before you. The curse is broken and the Land of Bondage will become the Land of Beauty once more. You are to be highly commended for all you have done."

Then the wizard raised his staff over the hudlunk and touched him on each shoulder.

"Helmud Hudlunk," he declared, "You have yet another great task before you. I am sending you back to proclaim this message of freedom throughout the land."

The wizard fastened the lantern around Helmud's neck and said, "This lantern will guide you in your journey."

"Furthermore," added the wizard, "I want you to know that the hunter who trapped your parents has discovered love and set them free. When you complete your journey, you will find them waiting for you. I will let them know that you are safe."

Helmud gave a happy growl. It sounded different than any growl Thomas had heard from him before. It was a truly friendly growl, not a scary one at all. The hudlunk's mane glowed in the light that flowed from the brightly shining lantern.

Next, the wizard looked at the boy. "And you, Thomas," he said. "As the lantern-bearer, you were the only one who could bring freedom to the Land of Bondage and you have done just that. We owe you a debt that we can never repay."

The wizard smiled gratefully at Thomas and spoke quietly, "It is time, though, for your return."

Thomas gazed once more across the chasm. The land looked brighter and more colorful and, somehow, it even felt freer. The boy savored the view and then turned to look at Helmud. Thomas realized just how much he would miss his friend.

As Thomas wrapped his arms around Helmud's neck, the wizard waved his staff across the sky.

In an instant, Thomas found himself standing in his bedroom back home. He was barefoot and dressed in his pajamas. It was just as dark outside as it was when he had first met the wizard. Thomas caught his breath in shock at his sudden return. It felt strange to be home.

His mother, hearing the noise, opened the door and found her son standing in the middle of the bedroom. She was quite surprised at the big hug he gave her.

"Are you alright?" she asked.

"I think so," Thomas replied, still trying to make sense of where he was. "I just went on an amazing adventure! A wizard sent me to another land and there was this creature named Helmud and a talking bug and . . ."

Thomas was still attempting to explain what happened when he felt his mother's hand on his forehead. Looking a bit worried, she said, "You don't have a fever. Maybe you just had a wild dream."

Thomas looked confused. The journey to the Land of Freedom had seemed so real. But now that he was back home in his own bedroom and wearing his own pajamas, the adventure did feel a bit too fantastic to be true.

After a moment, Thomas sighed, "Maybe you're right. Maybe it was only a dream."

"Well," said his mom, "let's get you back to bed, Okay? School is in just a few hours."

"Okay, mom."

Thomas got into bed and snuggled under the covers. As he pulled his blanket up around his neck, he discovered a toy that he had never seen before. Grabbing it tightly, Thomas held the stuffed animal close to his chest. Others would say that it looked ugly, but Thomas always treasured the furry animal with a dog's body, lion-like head and the name *Helmud* sewn on its tag.

Back Home

The Author

Kevin Grenier is the author of several books, including the *Legends of Crandor* series (legendsofcrandor.com). *Thomas and the Lantern* was written as a way to explore the true meaning of freedom in life. Kevin and his wife, Lisa, live in Colorado. They have six children.

The Illustrator

Terry Herb was born in 1969 in Thailand. He is a natural artist who has sold over 2,500 individual pieces and illustrated three books. He loves fishing, cooking and being in the outdoors. Terry currently lives in Southern California and he has three children. Terry's website is www.hirethisartist.com.